Relegation of Religion

By DG

Relegation of Religion

DG

Published by DG, 2025.

RELEGATION OF RELIGION

First edition. September 28, 2025.

Copyright © 2025 DG.

ISBN: 979-8231814305

Written by DG.

26/12/2025

To John

Health and happiness for the year ahead!

I hope you give this book a read and an understanding.

Yours

Dáire.

Also by DG

Capital of Spies
Stalkers Paradise
Democracy is Dead
Relegation of Religion

INTRODUCTION

Throughout mankind's existence, religion has played a key role in the development and maturity of the individual.

However, with the birth of the consumer society, the central role that religion once played has been greatly watered down to the extent that most modern day societies and their people seem lost an cast adrift in a world that is more complicated and at the same time soulless.

This book delves into the complications, the reasons for religions downgrade and dilution and see if this has been justified and required for man to evolve into his next evolutionary step.

CHAPTER 1

There are many names that I could give this book such as relegation, rediscovery or the decentralisation of religion but this book is to address the three major faiths or religions in the world which have the most followers, has the most influence on economics and global policies or has the most contentious history with gaps, question marks and faith based on tenuous beliefs or retelling of old stores in a different light to gain followers and inhibit influence in the world.

There is no doubt that man has used the other religions, and they are in fact spin off from the three major religions of Christianity with focus on Catholicism, Islam, and Judaism.

This book is not written to offend any followers of these religions but to give a perspective and honest assessment of their place in the twenty first century and whether their foundations and beliefs still whole up in the information age and whether we can still honestly believe that their teachings are still relevant to the vast majority of the world population.

So why draft a book about a topic when so many aspects of the topic have been covered in detail already through scholars of these religions and other intellects have conducted painstaking research into the background of these religions.

The simple answer is that the basis of all religions is to spread the beliefs and ideologies of these religions to gain followers and new believers.

These beliefs lead to cultural difference and the creations of different countries and territories. But the fact is that all these religions share remarkably similar beliefs and ideologies yet when they sit side by side either territorially or in a room, this is the cause of great conflict often leading to armed conflict and war.

So is it simply that religion real aim is to extend its power base at the expense of other religions and beliefs or is it simply that once we adopt a religion over another, we become blinkered to everything else round us and are unable to see the wood from the trees.

We buy into the beliefs of a specific religions and are unwillingly to accept any other argument or belief of another religion or sect.

This is the basis of the book.

Why with so many people invested in one religion over another is their so much conflict in the world. Are we all just a bunch of hypocrites spouting of the learnings and teaching of one religion without fully understanding their merits or their place in the world.

I for one have grown up in a country where religious beliefs have had and continue to influence the political policies of the country's political parties and the religious divide between the religions of Catholicism and Protestantism.

Both religions brought to this country by their followers who change the belief system from paganism to Christianity in a few hundred years.

So why would the people of a country choose one religion over another especially when the existing beliefs in pagan gods were handed down by their parents and grandparents.

The desire of people in the twenty first century to convert to other religions at the risk of alienising themselves from their existing social structure is increasing.

What are people getting from these conversions and why is their newly adopted religion giving them that their existing belief does not have or does not give them.

Sometimes these coverts go down destructive paths such as terrorism, and this conversion is to support their political belief as opposed to their spiritual beliefs.

Other religions such as Buddhism and Sikhism are more based on spiritual beliefs as opposed to the followings of a specific prophet or religious figure.

Budda the central figure in Buddhism does leave us a set of beliefs but these beliefs are based on the elevation of a person spiritual awareness and understanding in the place in the universe as opposed to organised religions and mass praying and organised group events often in sync with calendar events.

This book will draw parallelism between the three major religions and critically assess their failings as well as their successes and see if their creation has had a positive effect on the intellectual teachings and maturity of the population at large.

Whether the world would have been better off if religion did not play any role in the development of an individual.

Instead, the only beliefs where the laws of science and how they uphold the universe as opposed to some man in the sky holding up everything and who's life work is the education of person below him.

RELEGATION OF RELIGION

All major religions have this central super figure who is immortal and strives to make the lives of his followers better.

I will look at this concept and whether it is still relevant and believable in this modern age or will newer religions based on the concept of a mother nature figure, an omni present force in everything that we do.

This contrasts with a figure who some will see present on the side lines cheering us on but giving little in the way of help or guidance but instead rules and beliefs thousands of years old.

Some of these beliefs have been used and abused by man for political, economic, and egocentric reasons since they were first written down.

This book will also delve into how religion has shaped the map of the world and effected and in some cases slowed down human development at the expense of human lives, destruction, and war, many for vain reasons or for reasons only known by a select few.

This book is written in the backdrop of the death of Pope Francis and the election of his successor by a secret ballot.

The largest organised religion in the world with followers in the billion and wealth also in the billions with their own country to rule.

How did one religion become so powerful over other competing and more time relevant religions and how has the catholic church been able to maintain a front and centre stage presence in the world against so many competing demands and political upheavals.

The off shoot of Christianity, which being protestants and all the various forms of interpretation has caused segmentation and power battles in the broader Protestant churches, all fighting for dwindling numbers of followers.

How has this evolved in the twenty first century and is the original argument for the creation of the Protestant church still relevant or will we witness the return of the Protestants church's back to the main Christian church.

CHAPTER 2

Is it time, for the benefit of belief and continuity of existence that these churches find common ground and a mechanism for the reunification of all branches of Christianity.

This would require all believers accepting their leader as Saint Peter as opposed to a political leader who may be of a different faith and belief or instead a leader voted into office by popularity as opposed to their spiritual faith and teachings and understanding or the teachings of their religion.

Judaism with its central roots now in Israel could be seen as the oldest of the three main religions and we will look at the question why Christianity is not Judaism is the most populous religion given that Jesus and his followers were Jewish.

Why did Jesus followers believe the need existed for the creation of a new belief system and religion given that his mother, the spiritual head of the modern-day Catholic church was Jewish.

Was it merely the Roman empire capitalising on the success of Jesus followers over that of Judaism or was Jesus' teachings so different than what existed and groundbreaking that it required the creation of a new religion.

Judaism has survived many assaults on its people and their beliefs, and their history is that of being a nomadic tribe looking for their spiritual home.

However, the core of Judaism is that they are god's chosen people and as such their spiritual home is internal as opposed to geographical based.

Weapons and walls are the tool of their enemy were as words and beliefs are the tools to be used by the Jewish people.

This message has been lost in the ether through time and conflict. The bottom line is the reason Judaism has been under sustained attack, and it is that other races want what Judaism have or had.

The is the main reasons for war. Not to enforce your beliefs over another race but instead to take the very essence and make up of that race, religion and set of beliefs.

So why cannot the religions of Judaism and Islam get along when both have their core base in the middle east. The reasons are not necessarily about religion but more politics and economics.

Both religions represent hugely different races and ethnicities, and their fundamental belief system is different however they do share the requirement that each religion espouses the requirement to live peaceful with other ethnicities and to live a good life.

We will explorer what commonalties exist between these religions and how common consensus can be reached that would hopefully lead to a more peaceful coexistence between both races.

We will look at whether religion is overvalued, oversold, over dependent upon external factors that it cannot be controlled and whether religion can be rebooted for the times that we live in.

Does anything need to be done with it, scaled up, scaled down, reworked, tweaked, or just rewritten for the modern age to make sense of all the competing requirements of any of the major religions.

Just because something has been around for thousands of years does not mean that we accept it blindly without at least questioning and understanding the fundamental beliefs of a religion.

This will raise some has tough questions about core beliefs of Islam, Christianity, and Judaism and if their decline could lead to the extinguishment of religion or instead the transfer of followers to other smaller religions or worse still to cults and cultish leaders.

If the decline or collapse of one of the world's major religions occurred what would the outcome look like.

Would there be political or economic instability in a country, region, or part of the world and what would the outcome be.

Is this something to be encouraged or stopped at any cost.

Could this be even imagined and has any plans been put in place by any world organisation for such an event.

This book is a pro versus con for religion in the world today and asks the question whether, have we outgrown religion?

In previous times, centres of powers were confined to castles, forts and cities with governing Kings, Queens, and Noble men.

However, religion has also created and influenced the running's of most countries in the world and their centres of power be it Rome, Jerusalem, or Mecca commands serious power over large sways of the population on this planet.

However, the power and influence go unchecked as many of the followers are seen as people of God and since God is the ultimate judge of man then only God can decide a person's fate.

And this thinking is still in existence today. This was very prevalent in the times when sexual abuse by priests and bishops of the catholic church was going on.

The response of the authorities and police was that the matter was to be handled by the church and holy see.

Priest were being moved to another diocese often to commit the same indecent acts repeatedly without any justices for victims or punishment for those committing these acts.

So is this not just abuse of power and control by those in power or was there something else going on.

The church believes that the priests were the victims, and these children were outing themselves onto the priest with little option but to commit these acts even if consent was allowed in the eyes of the law this was an illegal act.

So, it was the laws of the jurisdiction that eventually led to these priests and bishops being sent to trial and not cannon law or the law of the church.

As far as the church was concerned, the Virgin Mary was pregnant, albeit by immaculate conception at aged twelve and therefore for most of the female population, pregnancy can only be achieved through sexual intercourse with a male.

The church never at any stage made it clear that the culture at the time in Palestine was that young girls did get married at a young age.

The age of twelve for a girl to be pregnant would have been acceptable but the fact that the pregnancy was outside wedlock would have been the main talking point of that day.

Now fast forward two thousand years and the reverse is true were a pregnancy to occur outside of marriage is normal but a girl to be pregnant would not only be a talking point, but it would also lead to the interventions of authorities and the punishment of those involved in the act of sex without consent.

So, a girl two thousand years ago could give consent for sex but today laws of most countries do not allow this to occur.

So does this argument supposed to explain sexual abuse by priests and bishops of children in the twentieth century. No, it is not but to show the shift in culture and explain the roots of Christianity and Catholicism today considering its development as a religion.

So why was a girl aged twelve picked to be the Virgin Mary. The reason was the age of a person who led a full life and died was a lot lower than today, some forty years lower or so.

And in that time a girl and women would be expected to produce as many offspring as possible as many children did not make it past there early years due to famine, war, and diseases.

So young girls upon commencement of menstrual cycle would have been expected to marry and produce children. This concept is the foundation of Christianity as Jesus born of a Virgin, son of God and prophet and went on to indirectly create a counter religion to Judaism.

As Jesus was rejected or simply not believed or accepted as the son of God, Judaism and Jews today rely on the teachings of the Old Testament while most Christians rely on the teachings of the New Testament.

So, if Jesus were accepted by Jews in his time, would Christianity have become the religion it is today.

It is likely that the world would be now made up of more people of the Jewish faith than Christians.

Christianity would have developed but nothing like what it is today.

CHAPTER 3

So is it that Jewish people missed out and are the architect of their own downfall and persecution.

The answers are most likely that Jesus did not fit into the teachings of Judaism and as Jewish people were seen as gods people and land promised to them by god, Jesus had a high bar to live up to and a difficult argument to win.

Even through his followers, his teachings, his works and miracles were not enough to convince the mainstay of the Jewish population that he was the future direction of the Jewish faith and not any previous prophets or even the great Moses who led the Jewish people out of slavery in Egypt to the promise land in Palestine, now called Israel.

As far as the Jewish people were concerned, Moses produced results were as Jesus talked a lot, made a lot of promises but if you are living in an arid dessert, you want more than hot air and fireworks.

You want results, you want something that you can physically touch and say that this is mine.

Jewish people are renowned for their wealth, work, and ownership with precious metals of gold and silver and precious stones of diamonds and Rubys.

These are items that hold their wealth and only increase with value over time.

These material goods is what Jesus was battling against and when he threw money changers out of the Temple this certainly did not help his standings in the Jewish community as he did not understand the concept that scales used in each transaction were an indirect reference to the weighing of a person's soul to get into heaven.

A main tenet of most religions.

God was the creator of these metals and stones, and their rarity increased their value and association with God.

So would there have been as much turmoil in the middle east if Judaism were the main religion in the world and not Christianity.

Let us have a look at the problem first. Jerusalem is the crossroad of the three main religion and most significantly the Temple Mount.

The western wall, the first temple of Judaism, Mohammeds accession into Heaven, the Al Aqsa Mosque and the birthplace of Christianity.

So why does one location, city and country have so much meaning for three of the major religions.

One of the reasons is that Jerusalem was a major trading post for many cultures two thousand years ago and the years that followed due to in part being part of the Roman empire.

Another reason is that it is argued that humanity began in Africa and soon migrated across into the Arabian Peninsula using a land bridge and up into modern day Egypt and Israel.

So, the occupations of these lands have been occurring for many thousands of years unlike other parts of the world which may have only been inhabited in more recent times.

But if Rome was the centre of the world at the time of Jesus's birth, why was he not born in Rome but instead in Palestine a lot more far removed from the seat of power and Caesar.

That is the main reason, for Jesus to try and influence in a city in which Caesar was not seen as God but as far as every roman was concern was God would have been a lot more difficult.

A birth in a Roman province would not be seen as a direct threat to the incumbent Caesar and would give Jesus more time to grow his power base.

Also, the Jewish people were being persecuted, and it may have been the intention that Jesus' presence would in some way curry favour with the region's governor and other tribal powers in the region.

However, this spectacular backfired and instead Jesus was swapped out for a convicted criminal, and crucifixion was the Jewish people appeasement to the region's governor during the Jewish religious holidays of Passover.

The Jewish people by that stage had enough of Jesus beliefs and teachings and realised that his presence was not only destabilising relationships with their Roman overlords and not helping them.

If Jesus really wanted to help his own people, he would just keep quite that he was the son of God and other totes to powers and instead become a follower of moses who links to God were well founded and unquestioned.

So, Jesus at the time, being a destabilising force, was his people Jewish, or of being birth through immaculate conception by a Virgin Mary of a different race of people completely different to the Jewish people.

He may have looked, acted, sounded Jewish, but the possibility is that Jesus may have come from a different race entirely.

Jesus is seen to be quite feminine in the way he conducted himself. He was no brute but quieter and gentler in approach and his teaching.

Though he did warn man eternal damnation in hell, he also toted heaven as the ultimate prize and place.

So, if Jesus was not Jewish, where was he from. And so, if angels were sent from heaven to help and guide Mary, they were not from Judaism version of heaven but instead from somewhere different entirely.

So was Jesus using the Jewish people to found his own religion and when he could not convince them, the only escape was self-sacrifice and execution.

This is an argument. It is no doubt that Jesus was put on earth to help the Jewish people, why else would he been there.

He was not there to help expand the Roman empire or the Egyptian empire.

His birthplace in a manger in a small village, miles from a large city of a humble birth was meant to draw in as many common people not of noble or religious birth into the teachings of Jesus.

As Mary and joseph were returning to their home village for a census by the Roman empire yet Mary ended up giving birth to a manger, none of Jesus or Marys family or friends did not help them out but instead they stumbled upon a manger.

Did Mary and Josephs family and friend forecast the troubles that this birth would bring and that was the reason they ended up in a manger.

No believable argument has been put forward to explain this reason other than that there was no room at the inn for them, that is they were not welcomed there.

The out of wedlock marriage really was a talking point and just like the days when unmarried couples could not stay in the same room in a hotel, this could have extended to the beliefs two thousand years ago.

CHAPTER 4

So is religion a sort of belief system that just automatically fills in the blanks of questions about the universe that we are unable to answer or unwilling for face.

There is no doubt that religious symbolism is based on the environment around us and the aspects of which we are unable to explain.

For example, the sun is the main proponent in any religion as the sun gives us light and day and is required for growth of crops and its associated harvest.

It is responsible for the season as its angle dictates the season and months and therefore gives us the ability to create time, clocks, calendar, and everything to do with horology.

As a result, the sun becomes the sun of God such is the power of the sun in people's lives.

So, religion piggy backs of this powerful tool that Mother Nature has provided us with and used to create a religion.

Remember Christianity is solely based on Jesus been accepted as the sun of God.

Once you accept Jesus as the sun of god which is required for Catholics in their first communion rite and again for their confirmation and reject any else that could be pertained to the have same or equal power, such as the devil, then you are on the side of good and the sun is good because it provides so many benefits to humans on Earth.

So is religion just leveraging the resources of mother nature for its own benefit and if so, what happened to the concept of mother nature and why is she not taking about for all the glory of her creations.

CHAPTER 5

Just like the concept of God, mother nature could be seen as an absentee landlord, which is he or she owns or has created all around us but other are exploring or exploiting these natural resources.

No argument exists between a direct relationship between mother nature and God that is one created and gave birth to the other.

They exist in their entirety as separate entities that exist in the same space. that is, no separation of duties, roles, and responsibilities and both are seen to have done the same job and therefore must take equal credit.

So why is the concept of God more front and centre than that of mother nature in which she seems only associated with weather and harvests and more a farming belief than a main stay belief.

The reason is that religion hides the fact that it is a business, a very profitable business that appeases the worries of the masses at their most crucial time in their lives, birth, death, marriage and transition from one point in their lives to another.

Mother nature, like most mothers is about stability and consistency such as the four seasons been delineated, the weather been normal for the time of the years and all things weather related.

So global warming is the enemy of mother nature as it is counter to what mother nature is about.

Not about change or new concepts and ideas but about predictability and the stability of the environment to support life and allow life as we know to grow and flourish.

So why has this happened. Religion as a business supports many jobs in the construction of churches, cathedrals, basilicas, schools, convents, and other religious institutions.

The contributions that believers and followers make goes directly back into these communities for their further expansion and thus acceptance into the societies that they became a part of.

God, it seems was able to pull the strings directly through his followers and economic activity flourished because of this policy.

It is like mother nature providing the hardware on which God and his followers were able to build upon with the concept of God getting all the credit.

But we must not forget who the real landlord is and how this relationship can be disturbed to the detriment of life on our planet, whether it is the shrinking of the polar ice caps, increase in desertification, overpopulated cities or the decrease of rural life.

Has the concept of God just gone too far and should we be aligning our belief system to that of mother nature than that of God.

Should we be more strongly associated with a mother figure than a father figure as this is where inequality exist in the world especially amongst the genders and the pay gap between males and their female counterparts.

If we followed a female figure would women be more likely to be in the driving seat, instead of man.

Although most religions do pay homage to senior female figure, they are more in the support role than in the decision making and leadership roles.

Is the unbalance in the world because of this unbalance in our belief system and that of the beliefs in the mortals that guide us from above.

So does a rebalancing of the universe need to occur for us to see a rebalancing in our societies.

This is already happening as we become more aware of our environment and the harmful things that we are doing to upset mother nature and the creations that she has given to us.

More people than ever before are trying to address this rebalancing of nature and their environment through the reduction of their carbon footprint and over reliance on fossil fuels and to the use of the free energy source of the sun.

The fact that solar power was overlooked for many years in favour of fossil fuels is a direct result of politics and big business ability to control a resource that is finite as opposed to the inability to control a resource that is abundant and free.

Only when the end of fossil fuels is near do we look around for an alternative that we know would have been able to do the job many years earlier for which the technology already existed for but for which was largely ignored as politics preferred to gain their energy for destabilised regions in the world such as the Middle East where most of the world's oil can be found.

So, it is fair to say that politician and big business people are not the friends of mother nature and prefer to ignore her for their own benefit and exploit her for all they can get and line their pockets with moneys from the fruits of her labour.

RELEGATION OF RELIGION

This is not a pleasant thing to say that a product of Mother nature would so much go against her wishes and desires but that is the fact of the situation.

Greed is good and bad behaviours are accepted which can only lead us to the conclusion that people who act like this are just badly behaved or brought up children whose parent were unable to educate their children in the ways of the world, somethings that is not required by a religion or legal system but is simply called good parenting.

If these behemoths of business had better parents may be the world would be in a better place and not like the way we have it, wars, famine, ecological disasters, hatred, racism and other nasty human traits that have crept in and that continue to exist in the world today.

So is bad parent the only reason for the turmoil that exists in the world.

CHAPTER 6

It goes to the heart of the religion of Judaism where Moses was asked to write down the ten commandments in which his followers must obey to be closer to God.

When Moses got down of the mountain, his followers were worshipping a golden cow. They had already made their decision, God was not for them, but this new belief, wealth and prosperity was for them.

They did not want to be living in hovels and tent all their lives, they wanted progress, change, economic activity, and if anything, God was only going to give them more of the same and nothing new. They would be better behaved but only for Gods gain and not for anybody else's.

This was God's way of lighting his load and responsibilities by pushing back on people to live a more rewarding live by threating each other with more respect.

This runs counter to business where to get ahead and stay ahead you need to be shrewd, smart, and not willing to take any prisoners.

Gods' belief that being nice to everybody was going to make the world a better place just did stack up to the Jewish people at the time.

So was God just uncoordinated for the people of the time.

It seems that something else creeped into the minds of the Jewish people of the time that change their minds from the time Moses went up mount Sinai to the time he came back with the written ten commandments.

Even today the value of the Ten Commandments in its original form would be beyond a value and price.

So why did the Jews of the day turn their back on God in such a blatant and belligerent way.

How did greed suddenly become the centre of their belief system.

That is a question that scholars are still trying to answer today but I would say that the lack of leadership for that critical junction in their existence was enough to tip them into another belief system were everything suddenly had a price and a place, and everything could be reevaluated in the context.

That is without somebody directly looking over everything that they did the Jewish people at the time devolved and forgot all Gods teaching and chose a different path for the growth and development.

The ways and laws of God was not going to bring them happiness but instead of the recentring of business in their lives would and as a result their society would be better off for it.

Even today Jewish people are a mainstay of the business world and are influential in their decision if not in banking, technology, pharmaceuticals as well as precious metals and stones.

Their relationship with business has not diminished as time has gone only but only got stronger and their relationship with their God could been seen in equal light.

The Jewish people have become a persecuted race through the centuries and one can only hope that it was not a result of their falling out with their God but instead the sharing of land with other races that is causing this renewed distaste with the Jewish race.

In my own home country, Israel has closed their embassy as a direct result of government criticism of how Israel is treating Palestine and the Palestinian people.

This is the diplomatic statement that a country can make to another country.

It says we no longer respect your opinions as it runs counter to our own policies.

To me it is sad to see a nation that is neutral and seen as a friendly nation to all around, for another nation to be cutting direct ties with that country. It cannot be a good thing.

So why does Israel choose to be so confrontational and so defensive about its political positions.

Israel always mixes politics, religion and military might and it does not see one as the extension of the other but merely the same thing but in a different guise.

Israel when offended will respond either politically, using the Jewish religion or propaganda and Israel being the home of the Jewish people or as we have seen increasingly in the last decade, the Jewish militarily position.

So, the closing of an embassy is the lowest position on the ladder that Israel can respond.

The reason for this mix is that Israeli people identify themselves through their religion first and then by where they come from.

RELEGATION OF RELIGION

This stems from the fact the Jewish race was a nomadic race as people from part of the world with large dessert, moving around in search of water, trade and arable land was part of their life.

The Egyptians enslave the Jewish race to build their pyramid in homage to their gods and to achieve immortality.

So, the Egyptian pharaohs used the fact the Jewish people where god's chosen people and from there, used their own pagan gods in concert to create the concept of immortality for each Pharaoh.

So even thousands of years ago, Jewish people were being used to create other countries or dynasties empires.

So why is this an occurring theme for the Jewish people.

In their eyes and other races eye they are seen to possess something that other races do not have and it is from this that other races try to dominate the Jewish race.

This is recognised by Israel and the Jewish diaspora, and it is from this that the Israeli government takes a no-nonsense approach to other cultures using bullying tactics, military might, or neighbouring countries gang up on Israel.

The fact that a land mass that is only seventy miles across can cause so much turmoil in the world leads me to believe that it is not about the territory but instead about the persons who inhabit or occupy the territory.

So even with the sudden change and awareness that Israel has about the potential for war to start at any moment, other countries and actors choose to annoy and bully Israel.

As far as most of the world sees it, Israel has historical attachment and ancient claims to the land and would have the oldest claims to the land amongst modern cultures and race that live or inhabit the land.

Therefore, the creation of Palestine, by the British was a political identity not a religious or cultural identity and it is from this that modern day cultures cling onto as ownership and entitlement to parts of the land that make up Israel.

So, the external actors who propagate war in this religion are external to the problem and located further afield than the middle east and more likely in Europe and the America's.

It is more likely that individuals and not necessarily any one government that is sponsoring terrorism in Israel.

CHAPTER 7

The recent October 7th incursions into Israel from the Gaza Strip has all the hallmarks of a private special force's organisation such as Blackwater.

This was not a band of Robin Hood like people deciding to upset their neighbours.

This operation was planned and financed from persons and organisation from further afield.

They choose a multiple pronged attack from a military strong point into its enemies' territories and killed and kidnapped its citizens.

Their target was not an Israeli military installation but instead the target was Israeli citizens.

Any aged citizens from babies to old age pensioners were kidnapped and brought back behind enemy lines.

They were used for publicity reasons and as ransom in exchange for Palestinian prisoners.

This is no different to the Nazi's in World War Two who created Getto's then concentration camps then the gas chambers.

And no doubt this is what Hamas wanted these captive Israeli prisoners to think.

As a prisoner, it must have been a horrible ordeal but as all Israeli citizens must go through military service, no doubt they were prepared for any eventuality like this.

So hence the strong defence that Israel puts on when any threat is made against its territory or its citizens.

CHAPTER 8

When the Jewish people were enslaved in Egypt, they were put to work building the large pyramids that we see today in the valley of the Kings and Luxor.

These landmarks that we know extremely well and not just tombs of dead Kings and Pharaohs but real proof that the Jewish people have been an enslaved race for thousands of years.

Post-World War Two, the Jewish people realised that their nomadic existence and lifestyle was no more and that they needed their own homeland.

Neven again to be reliant on the good nature of races that they should not trust in the first place, even if they represent the upper echelon and wealth class in the country from which they are living.

This only creates jealousy and animosity amongst the race and culture that they are living in.

The creation of a new country would result in a drop of class but for the Jewish race it is better to have a place they can call home than a country they call their house.

Little did anyone realise that the creation and existence of Israel would be fraught with difficult, dangers, unrealised risks, and worst still hidden enemies, which is two faced followers and friends.

People who were pretending to be friends of the Jewish race and Israel but were secretly plotting its downfall and destruction.

We only must look at the Munich Olympics in 1972 to see how this two-face culture became known.

There can be little doubt the German officials and government were behind this as they were the ones who had the most to gain from manufactured terrorism from a group that nobody heard of gaining entry to a supposedly secure location and killing and holding to ransom Jewish people.

The same story repeats itself whether its thousands of years ago or in the twenty century, Jewish people being killed or held to ransom to the benefit of another race or culture.

It would be logically given the history of relationships between Germany and the Jewish people, as Israel, that Germany would have at least the Israeli part of the Olympic village secure if not like today the whole village and area around it.

Germany used security guards, reminiscent of the concentration camps of World War two instead of police and military.

When trouble occurred, there was no special forces prepared or trained to deal with the situation, and no call was made to any neighbouring country for them to deploy their special forces.

Germany's surrender terms in World War two did not bar them from protecting their own people or visiting people so on an extremely basic level Germany look incompetent if not complicit.

It is unlikely that Germany would be allowed to hold another Olympics and questions remain as to how they were awarded the 1972 Olympics in the first place.

Other actors would need to be at play for this to occur and the holding captive of Israeli athlete was the end game for this awarding to Germany of the Olympics in the first place.

This may be a cynical view but not held without some deep sceptics and cynicism of the Germany race and their intentions.

Even today, Germany has nothing to be arrogant about and should remember their history and understand their personal traits instead of playing back-room politics with other countries territories and citizens.

At the end of the day, countries who could be bothered, it would not take much to invade and occupy Germany and to put them under a cloud from which they could not continue their invasion into other nations lives.

This type of politics, hand in hand with religion, remember Germany is the home of Protestants and we see how its effects cause century old wars in the north and south of Ireland.

The fact that a German citizen took on the Christian church, the Catholic church today and created a breakaway religion that went on to massacre seven million Jews, we must raise the fact that the German race has and had intentions to take over the world through the means of ethnic cleansing.

CHAPTER 9

The excuse provided by rebellious Germans was that the church at home was corrupt and that merely replacing one Pope with another was not going to solve the problems as the church's problems were too deep routed that only the creation of a breakaway religion based on the teachings of Christ and no one else's interpretation was going to solve the problem.

And that is what occurred but instead of getting one religion you got many distinct types and interpretations of beliefs being born into existence.

Each with subtle differences but all the same different forms of Protestant with various places of worship often backed by a rich benefactor.

Today if the same thing were to occur, we would call these breakaway religions as cults with cult followers and would display all the hallmarks of a cult.

That is were people would live and work in the same community and world for companies and socialise in places that were directly owned by the church or by followers of the church who were chosen by the church hierarchy to be front and centre and as a role model for the church.

This can be seen by the religion of Mormon in Salt Lake City Utah, U.S. and by scientology based in California.

These religions were set up by persons who did not believe or did not want to believe the followings of the Christian church and instead set up their own religion and gathered their own followers.

It is almost like an a la carte approach or cheery picking approach to a religious belief, in that we will take the best bits like miracles, after life, being born again and forgiveness and forget about the other bits which aren't a seller.

It is giving the people what they want as opposed to what they need.

Eternal damnation is a tool used to scare followers as opposed to warn followers against the dangers of ignoring god's law.

And so, religion becomes a business and not a form of redemption as Jesus taught is follower as.

Forgive and love god and all is good instead of forgiving and love the other followers and all will be good.

CHAPTER 10

So why is there such a close association with religion and the worship of a god, violence, and war, such in theory should be opposites.

The bottom line is that most modern-day religions only have room for one god as opposed to the gods of Greece and Rome were gods represented distinct aspects of human life such as harvest, rains, the seas, and war itself.

These gods were pitted against each other and where perpetuals in dispute with one another.

The fact that they were related did not matter, in fact it made things worse.

This type of behaviour eventually made its way into the lives of ordinary people to whom would have a favourite god or temple that they prayed.

As such as people made their allegiance to one God over another and this created division not unity amongst people.

People choose to live near their god's temple thus creating a geographical division which could create an economical division depending on if the god had rich benefactors or not and as such if the temple was located in a rich part of a town or city.

Its roots simple but the long-term damage that this type of God structure created was long term and resulted in riots and public disorder amongst citizens of a town or city.

As such the architects of modern religion choose to go with one supreme being as opposed to a large family of gods such as the Olympians or Titans in Greek classical civilisations.

This removed division of power in exchange for division of labour.

For example, in Christianity, God sent his son to earth to be born out of wed lock by immaculate conception.

Each person in the story had a role and responsibility and did not go beyond that role.

Joseph helped Mary with the birth and the three wise men acknowledged that Jesus was the son of God.

It is from this simple beginning that Christianity flourished.

It kept the root basics simple so as not to confuse followers of who is what.

The only complication comes when some followers believe that Jesus is in fact god and not just the son of God.

This then asks the question if Jesus is God, then does the holy Trinity not exist anymore or was it just a temporary state of existence for God.

So, this means that God status can change and flux depending on the situation at hand.

This flies in the face of religion in which a central higher being is fixed and permanent in people's minds. To try and upset the apple cart by over complicating a simple structure gives way to people turning away from the religion.

The fact is Jesus was sent into the world at the behest of God his father to move the central immortal face of religion from a female figure, who through her actions created original sin, to a male figure, who acknowledges eve's wrongdoing.

Jesus not only accepts his own short coming but takes responsibility as such for eve's sins so that people can get into heaven again.

This is the reason Saint Peter is the gate keeper to heaven and hence the name of Saint Peters Square in Rome.

His symbol of the fisherman's ring that each successive Pope wears in Saint Peter's hold up the two keys to heaven.

Only because God sent Jesus to earth to reset relations between man and God could people start re-entering heaven after Adam and eve were banished from the garden of Eden.

Before Jesus arrival on earth Judaism did not hold a heaven in any high regard and the pagan gods of Rome and of Greece only had a heaven for the existing Gods, that being Mount Olympus, and only mortals who had shown true courage, wisdom or belief could expect to join the Gods in heaven.

So, for the average person, heaven was out of reach for them, and this was also the case for Egyptian Gods, where an afterlife was only available for pharaohs and king and their followers and animals who were also buried with them and who they would need in the afterlife.

CHAPTER 11

So why did Christianity decide to make heaven a possibility for all their followers.

The bottom line is that it made good business sense. Why not.

If people lead a worthy life and follow the rules as set down by God and Jesus and his disciples when it came to being judged and if a person's soul as pure then they could expect entry into heaven and paradise.

This thought was too good for many Christians to let go and may followers of Jesus and his disciples change their ways, lives, and teachings to become a better person to be guaranteed a spot in heaven.

So, Saint Peter being the first pope and the successive lines of popes since then are the gate keepers to heaven where heaven is seen as Saint Peters Basilica in Rome and the gates of Saint Peters Basilica are in fact the gates to heaven.

However, to see them in their real guise we must move from our mortal state from our bodies and in fact the only entry that can get into heaven is our soul in its purest form.

We must leave behind our bodies as a reminder to others of our mortality, for those to morn our loss and to pray for our souls to get into heaven.

So, what is the backup plan for those people not good enough to get into heaven but repent their sins.

Purgatory, the waiting room.

Most people do not live a pure and fulfilled life; there are gaps or sins or turning their back on God and simply repenting does not guarantee anything.

So, heaven does have a holding area called limbo which was original created for unbaptised babies who had not sinned but were born of sin because of original sin.

They had done nothing wrong but could not get into heaven because of original sin.

So, limbo has now been reinterpreted as a sort of holding area where people are given time to undo the wrong doings of their previous life which will prepare them for entry into heaven.

This has been successfully interpreted by Hollywood film studios and has created many films based on this concept.

So, this means that the average person does not have to be perfect throughout their whole lives but instead can turn their lives around and make good on their short falls and wrong doings.

So, in the space of a few thousand years, heaven has gone from a place for the elites to a place for the average person.

So, this would mean that heaven would need to expand in space for place for all these new entries.

So, heaven has gone from a temple or large area that would seat twenty or thirty people, to a place that would not only seat millions of people but also a place that would support millions of people.

With the evolution of heaven from its basic concept to its present-day belief, you are talking about a floating city high in the skies.

So, the original concept did not have any worries about the expansion of heaven where the present version of heaven has all the worries that a modern city might have.

So has lowering the bar to heaven been a clever idea all round or did we simple just bottle up all our problems to be opened and responded to later.

This is the case, that yes, we want people to lead a life with God in their lives but at the same time not much thought was given to this policy change and the logistics around it.

CHAPTER 12

And bottling up our problems is just what happened, and this policy change led to the reformation and the split in the Christian church into Catholics and protestants, both followers of Jesus Christ but who differed over the entry requirements into heaven.

Protestant believed this lowering of the bar was not good for the church as a whole and the selling of indulgences by Bishops, which was basically a backstage pass into heaven was doing long term damage to the church and its followers and if this practise was not changed then something was going to happen.

The reformation period and the split of the Christian church into Catholicism with its headquarters in Rome and into different versions of protestants from Anglican to Lutheran based on a particular person's interpretation of the Bible did not do any good for the followers of Jesus Christ.

In fact, it further diluted the teaching and message of Jesus into something that was more political than spiritual.

The message that Jesus was sent by God to deliver us from evil had got lost along the way and what we were left with was second or third hand information, beliefs and teachings by a person who was maybe fifteen hundred years away from knowing Jesus.

The disciples of Jesus were the only people that Jesus trusted to deliver his message to the world in his absence, and this is no more obvious by the guests who were invited to the last supper.

The last supper, Jesus last meal on earth before his crucifixion was attended by his disciples and it is from this meal that modern church services are drawn from.

Readings, communion and listening all form the main part of church services for Christians around the world and has been for the last two thousand years.

This is where Jesus explains the concept of life and afterlife through him and with him.

Only by believing in Jesus and Jesus alone will you be guaranteed entry into heaven.

The breaking of bread and drinking of wine are symbols of Jesus's body and blood and by the crucifixion of Christ will this become true, and the sins of eve will be purged.

Belief in anybody else will not guarantee you this passage.

As such everything from this point on is based on Jesus and all the disciples are doing is broadcasting this message around the world.

This is a fact that was overlooked during the reformation period.

Even if the church was selling indulgences, it is plain as days that only by following Jesus's teachings will we get into heaven.

So, the problem was not about corruption in the church but just like the Romans who replaced their own pagan gods in favour of Christianity, this concept was seen as powerful and many people wanted to hop on the bandwagon especially in time when death rates were quite high due to war, disease, the black death and famine.

People were in sorts looking for a life insurance policy and the selling of indulgence was the life insurance policies that people wanted.

So, it seems that religion just like any institute that is established by man is open to abuse regardless of their intentions when they set out our if to do gods work or just to improve the planet that we share and the culture and way of life that we follow.

Every religion at some time has fallen on its own swords, whether it is child sexual abuse in the Catholic church, Nepotism in the Protestant church, Corruption in the Mormon church or Terrorism in the religion of the faith of Islam.

So why is this so and would we be just be better of not having religion at all.

The fundamental belief is that God not only created good but also created evil and this is what religion in society acknowledges.

No government department or agency or any other establishment bar religious institutes recognise this fact and so just like as most religious beliefs goes, God created everything and from everything good as well as evil was born or created.

With this argument is that if everything came from God that God must in some way or part be evil also or even Satan is the representation of all that is evil then God at some stage whether in this universe or a previous one finished of Satan and from this inherited Satan's evil and from this God created evil or an extension of evil.

With this, Satan at some level must have been a prodigy or spawn of God, an offspring a son or daughter who went rogue and did not follow in the ways of God.

The modern context of evil and Satan and lucifer is that is that Satan was a fallen angel from heaven who was kicked out of heaven for not bowing to Adam as God creation of a perfect man.

Satan must have felt that he was been gazumped by Adam and in some way had fallen out of favour with God.

CHAPTER 13

Let us break this observation down into a simple argument.

If your father suddenly came home with a new puppy, without warning, and said this creation of mine is now man and you must all bow to this puppy.

Given that you are an angel, born in heaven, with the power of flight and mortality and suddenly this creation shows up and you dad says now bow before thee, you would be right to think that your dad has lost his marbles.

If he is not willing to see this or understand this and after no doubt an argument you have a falling out with him, you are most likely going to leave the family home and anyone who is of the same belief and can see what is coming down the line will do the same.

This could be seen as insanity and for you own safety and comfort you are going to go your own separate way.

The fact the lucifer, the bearer of light, which means the enlightened one should be painted in such a light by the scriptures is a bit of a cover up and Gods followers trying to paint God making the correct decision and lucifer the one in the wrong.

The fact to this day that followers of the Christian beliefs are unable or unwilling or afraid to separate out these pieces of information and come to their own conclusion means that the Christian church has done a very good job of mislabelling who were the good actors and who were the bad actors in this fall from grace for such a central figure of the old testament.

Unfortunately, this decision by God to throw lucifer, the enlightened one out of heaven, just like eve was thrown out of Eden, was wrong and they were both made escape goats.

It is likely that Adam was the one who ate the apple from the tree of knowledge not eve, the women getting blamed for man's failings is still issues that occur even to this day.

On a side note, why do women get paid less that men for doing the same job and the same or more hours in work.

Is it a result of original sin and women to this day are getting blamed for eve's action or more likely Adam's action.

CHAPTER 14

So why do we think that it was Adam and not eve that was the creator of original sin.

Adam's entry in heaven according to the scriptures was already controversial as it resulted in the kicking out of the enlightened one or intelligent one from heaven.

As God saw him as perfection, Gods' decision was that Adam must go forward and multiply.

As such Adam was placed in the garden of Eden and God created eve from one of Adams ribs hence the term floating rib.

Eden was not heaven but paradise on earth. If God really thought Adam was perfection surely, he would have left him in heaven and not brought him down to earth or Eden to propagate.

This would mean that Adam was made and not created.

In the celestial terms there is a significant difference between being created and being made.

Think of creation as using the matter of the universe to create a body or object were as being made is using what parts are lying around to make something for a specific purpose.

An object that is made has a specific purpose or role were a creation comes into existence to the universe.

Adam being brought down to Eden is really a step down as God knew he was no match for what was still left in heaven so in order to save face, he brought Adam down in Eden, a walled garden, a safe space to propagate with eve and spawn a generation of humans.

The fact the Adams place in the scriptures is at the expense of Lucifer, who goes on to be labelled as the evil one, must mean that Adam should be the opposite of Lucifer and all that is righteous and good.

However, the story does not go that way and as original sins come into fruition, Jesus must be sent from the heaven to restore order after civilisation goes into turmoil with the movement towards cities of sin such as Sodom and Gomorrah.

So, it seems gods decision to kick lucifer out of heaven created a downward spiral effect for humankind, something we have yet to recover from.

But going back to why we think Adam was to blame for original sin and not eve, as eve was made using one of Adams ribs, and eve being the representation of womenkind, even to this day, at the very least eve is a offspring of Adam, where Adam is a representation of God.

In the garden of Eden, it is said that a serpent, which is the devil in disguise, tempts eve to eat the fruit of the tree of knowledge as she was hungry.

Eden is represented as a garden with boundless fruits and other food groups which eve could eat from.

To say that eve was hungry and that was why she ate from the tree seems to be stretch of the truth.

Also, it is said that eve tried to encourage Adam to do the same and not eat from the tree does not really stack in a modern representation of man.

CHAPTER 15

Today man is seen with many faults and is easily affected by temptation.

Women as the primary caregivers and progenies of the next generation are more likely not to be swayed by temptation and be 'good' as opposed to man who are more easily tempted into doing things that they should not be doing in the first place.

Women make many sacrifices to have children, a lot more than men do, and it is through these sacrifices that women learn about restraint and controlling their temptation and urges.

Were as man in the modern context does not have the same level of societal restrictions from which they can learn about discipline and control.

There are more open to the elements and therefore temptations.

The appearance of the serpent in the garden of Eden was no doubt a test by God to see how far man or women had evolved.

If man was to be seen as the one from which original sin came from, then they would always be seen as week and not easily be able to control.

However, if women were to be seen as from were original sin evolved from, and women to this day called the weaker sex, then they could be more easily controlled given that women have a lot less physical presence than man.

It would be a lot more believable if it were eve and not Adam who ate from the tree of knowledge.

The tree of knowledge was a representation of God on earth just like we see Jesus on the cross. God and gods' representation on earth.

The fact that eve was an extension of Adam does not matter in this instance.

Adam realised that he has been demoted from heaven and thought that the only way back to heaven is to become moral and godly and to eat from the tree of knowledge.

His belief may have been that just like from Jesus and the last supper and holy communion, by eating that what is a representation of god, from the last supper, bread for his body and wine for his blood, Adam may have seen the tree of knowledge as the brain of god, that which contained all the knowledge of god on earth and by eating or ingesting a part of the tree, that is the fruit, or offspring, or seeds of the tree then Adam would come god or god like.

Once Adam had ingested the fruit of the tree then Adam would ascend into heaven and would again be brought into the folds of heaven, a heaven through which he brought turmoil through his existence.

When this did not materialise then Adam was left with no option than to blame eve and could have made the story up of the serpent to get back at lucifer for not bowing to him when they were both in heaven.

The facts or writings or the teachings lay all the blame solely on eve where it would have been Adam with all to gain from eating from the tree of knowledge and not eve.

Adam may have been a made apple all along and once God realised this demoted him to Eden.

In Eden he decided to test him and when he blamed eve and not owned up to the infraction himself.

CHAPTER 16

God knew then all of humankind was domed.

If you cannot get the foundations for a house right, then everything that is built on top of it will be weak, unstable, and able to topple over at the drop of a hat.

It is why today that the Pope in Rome is the seat of Saint Peter.

Remember Saint Peter denied knowing Jesus and being associated as a follower of Jesus to save his own hide, instead of being the seat of Adam or eve, from which all descendant of humankind came from.

God realised that the only way that mankind can save itself is not through the intervention of God, which already proved to have disastrous effects, but for man to come to the realisation and understanding of the limits of its own existence and not try to be God but to live a life and way that God would wish for them.

However, the painting of Lucifer, or the enlightened one as the root of all evil will only slow this march of man to leave the world of ignorance and false truths and enter a world of honesty and an existence that is of benefit to the world that man exists in and the environment of that world.

So, the argument of Adam and eve still resonates to this day, and their action may be seen to contribute to the disfunction that the world is currently experiencing.

For women, the primary caregiver of a family unit to be portrayed in such a poor light so far back in printed text is a position that women have yet to extract themselves from.

And this is a position that God of the Christianity religion has put women in.

In Islam eve is reference but women are not held in such a poor light, and it is the media sent to such countries as Afghanistan that is portraying Muslim women in such a poor manner.

Information and news about women being beaten and raped is inaccurate.

For them their god has laid down rules which women and men must abide by and if these rules are broken then the repercussions can be great, and by great yes death by stoning, banishment and forced marriage are consequence which is meant to bring warry women back in line.

As women are seen as the weaker sex, they must be periodically brought back in line when they stray.

The Islamic religion is unforgiving in this and countries under rule of Sharri law are even more under the spotlight and women are watched and checked to see that their behaviour meets the standards set down to them by their god.

Women are seen as the primary caregivers in the Muslim family unit and for them to propagate the next generation they must be clean and pure in body, mind and thought.

Their bodies are only seen as a vessel from which the spirit inhabits and for the spirit to be kept pure, then their body and mind must be kept clean and pure.

Any deviation will cause a downward spiral of the behaviour of an individual which could lead to further consequences for the family unit and society in general.

That is why at the first sign of this behaviour the punishment is so severe to stop this behaviour creeping into other people's behaviour and becoming accepted practise.

So, it is not that Muslim women are looked down by their male counterpart but instead elevated and kept at an elevated position as their role in Muslim society is seen as important and uncompromising at the same time.

So how Muslim text interprets eve's original sin is not to justify or even understand but instead to set-up warnings in their societies to stop this behaviour from occurring in the first place or spilling over into other parts of society.

So is they being anyway that eve can be exonerated from the guilt of original sin or are all women faithed to follow the path that eve created.

If eve is indeed an escape goat for Adams betrayal to God, then history has been told to cover up Adam's infraction and this is a difficult story to be retold in a different light even if reinterpreted or understood given different facts or scenarios.

We can only try to educate ourselves to escape ignorance and try to better ourselves through religion in other parts of lives.

CHAPTER 17

However, in a religious context and as followers of Christianity, we must accept Jesus' reason for being sent into the world in the first place which is one of the main tenets of Christianity.

Christianity requires that we accept Jesus and that in some instances supersedes eve as he was born without original sin through the immaculate conception.

The immaculate conception was god's way of resetting the dial on Christianity and Judaism.

Judaism shunned eve because of original sin and the main thrust of Judaism is Moses who brought the Jewish people out of Egypt where they were enslaved into the promised land that God had promised to them, as sons of David.

Many religions have turning points that shape all beliefs after a point and in the mind of Jewish people, Moses exodus from Egypt to the promised land, under the noses of a compliant king and pharaoh means that Moses was in dialogue with God as no other leader previously could achieve the same result.

So, what does these points in major religions do with the modern world and how are we are positioned in the modern world.

Belief is a powerful set of rules from which are handed down from one generation to the next and guide us in our everyday lives.

Religion for many defines their culture, identity, beliefs, where they are geographically located in the world, lives, and their place in the world.

Religion is borderless and extends across huge sways of territory on our planet.

Major religions cover known territories, and the birthplace of a religion is normally where that religion is most powerful and dominant.

For example, the middle east for Islam, the west for Christianity, Israel for Judaism, India for Hinduism, although other religions do make their ways into all countries in the world, they normally hold the ground from which that religion evolved from.

In many countries democracy took second place to the religious heads of the country's religion, and this still runs through today in such countries as Iran and Egypt.

Revolutions were guided by religious persons as opposed to military persons.

However, in many other countries the power of churches and synagogues and mosques is waning as many countries are possible seeking the western way of life, drop their core beliefs or worse still substitute their core belief for another culture's beliefs much to the detriment of the society's fabric in that country.

Religion which plays a beacon light in many societies, a safe place or a steadfast guide for future direction is no longer the same which may explain the rise of fundamentalist leaders, leftish politics, racism, bigotry and other parts of human behaviours which was kept under wraps or manged for so many years.

Not that this behaviour ever completely disappeared from the human traits but instead was not so common and its existence did not have a justification for being so present and obvious in society.

CHAPTER 18

People's beliefs shaped the societies that they lived in and for many still do but people do not seem to have much self-control over their desires and act out every temptation as if not doing so will mean that they are missing out on some aspect of life that will contribute positively to their overall well-being and happiness.

For many people it is like they do not have an off switch or do not have the ability to say no to what they know will be harmful or damaging for them in the short term or long run.

At each junction they are giving into their internal desires and temptation, throwing caution to the wind and unaccepting of the damages of their behaviour will bring to themselves and to the society that they live in.

This behaviour does not have a shelf life or is not confined to a period of time in their lives but instead when people get onto these paths it is actually the decline of an individual and their value to society diminishes and their eccentricities of their behaviour becomes worse and worse and their decline becomes more and more obvious.

People do not possess a natural brake or stop gap to prevent their decline in their behaviour.

It is not something innate to them but instead something that must be taught and learnt by everyone that inhabits the earth.

And this is the gap that religion fills.

That is, it is through teaching or learning that we go through to better ourselves as an individual.

The religion that we are born into is normally the set of rules and guidelines that we follow that makes up for our inadequacies.

Eve's original sin was god's way of showing us that remember you are only human after all and should not in any way just because you were created by God does not mean that you are God but instead followers of God.

The dilution into humans seeing themselves as God or God like comes to the fore in religious off shoots such as cults were one person, a self-appointed leader has other people believe that he is God and everyone else must listen and follow what this person says and does.

These people slowly and over time have become brainwashed by this person.

What this person has done has people to see in him something that only they can see in this person.

Smoke screens and mirrors, a performer, an entertainer but a person who knows how to manipulate others around and get them to do exactly what they want them to do.

These people are extremely dangerous and the end game for cults is mostly the same.

When they run out of new material or when they run out of tricks, they start to get rid of the non-believers one by one either individually or collectively.

These types of people are selfish, show no empathy and are only interested in power and power over people.

The role that cults have played has destroyed people lives is well known and covered in many fact-finding documentaries, but you must remember Jesus breakaway from Judaism was seen in those days as a cult or displaying cultish behaviour, not of belief in a pagan god but a reinterpretation of the relationship between the Jewish people and God.

So, the fact that Christianity was born from Judaism and exceeds Jewish followers by the billions, even when originally seen as a cult must question what was so different between how Jesus was portrayed and how other more modern religion leader, some with cultish tendencies are seen by their follower, by the media and by government agencies.

The answer lies in how emperor of Rome saw the waning support that Roman gods commanded and the rise of follower of Christianity who were promised an after life if they followed Jesus's teachings.

For the Caesar in Rome, it was an easy and cheap win. They did not have to do anything but rebadge their existing temples and places of worship such as the Pantheon in Rome to Christianity.

Even some of the symbolism was the same.

It meant the Caesar could be head of the church, head of the army and head of the political establishment.

This made the Caesar a far more powerful and dangerous person to foreign and domestic enemies and to anyone looking to steel his power base.

CHAPTER 19

For the three major religion, one day a week is dedicated to worship, the sabbath.

For Christians it is Sunday, for Muslims it is Friday and for Judaism it is Friday to Saturday, dusk to dusk.

Special emphasis is placed on this day for worship, prayer, and attendance to respective place of worship.

In recent time for Christianity this emphasis has become less.

Though people still observe the Sabbath, the numbers of people attending Sunday service and mass has steadily been dropping off with churches amalgamating and closing and parish priests covering ever wider areas.

Less businesses close for the Sabbath and the days when all businesses closed for Sunday is long gone with convenience and consumerisation ruling over faith and observance.

For Judaism and the state of Israel, the Sabbath is observed more than in Christianity and shops and business do close and public transport is curtailed.

People are expected to observe the Sabbath, however this is more a political decision than and spiritual decision, as less people on the street during these times means less chances of a terrorist attack.

However, this is not always the case during large religious festivals such as the Passover.

In the Muslim world, the Sabbath again is more strictly observed, and businesses and shops do close for the period of worship.

This is both a spiritual and political decision depending on which Muslim country you are living in or visiting.

For businesses in the three major religions countries, the work week is defined by what day the sabbath falls on.

In Israel, the work week begins on a Sunday as the sabbath ends on the Saturday evening.

In Christian countries the work week begins on a Monday as the sabbath ends on the Sunday night.

RELEGATION OF RELIGION

In Muslim countries, the Sabbath ends on Friday night and the Saturday is a normal working day, with the only exception being Muslim territories in Israel, such as the west bank and Gaza strip where migrant workers must follow the Jewish work week as opposed to the Muslim work week.

The influence that religion plays in these religious based societies is still there, but it is more historic than relevant.

Goods and service can still be purchased on these Sabbath days with the age of twenty-four seven commerce and the internet, and as such the emphasis on one day a week set aside for the worship of their god is lost.

Now each day becomes more blended into the earlier one with no break or distinction between one workday and another, where one workday end and another begins.

Now its increasing becoming more and more the same and in order for become to break with the hum drum of normality, you have more and more people taking short breaks, using their long weekends such as bank holiday, and more foreign travel than ever before.

If the Sabbath was left as it was, with the vast majority of shops and business closing for this day, people would have a natural mental reset for the next working week instead of a day, where shops, roads and parks are as busy as any other day.

The Sabbath for the three major religions is quite similar, in that it is about visiting a place of worship, normally located in the area where you live, sharing a meal with family members, and slowing down and relaxing for the day, with no one priority overshadowing your time.

This whole meaning, habit and existence has been lost for most people, with what the older generations are the ones still understanding and respecting the need for the Sabbath.

CHAPTER 20

A lot of this change can be contributed to the over commercialisation of the two major Christian religious festivals of Christmas and Easter, which is a celebration of the birth and resurrection of Jesus.

For most commercial entities, the further dilution of the meaning can be seen, how for some this is referred to the holiday period instead of Christmas, which for some Christians is an insult.

Christmas for Christians is about a message of hope in the form of a child who brings peace and prosperity to the world.

The giving of gift is loosely based on the offerings the three wise men gave to Jesus, which happened a number of days after the birth of Jesus and who followed a star to Jesus' manger.

This has been interpreted by the commercial world as a reason to place the whole gift giving aspect on the day that Jesus was born on as opposed to the days after Jesus's birth.

This further dilutes the meaning of Jesus birth to the world and instead of a celebration of life, it has become a celebration of commerce, with the emphasis shifting to the three wise men as opposed to the holy family.

So why does commerce become so intertwined and engrained in Christianity.

Some people may refer to Jesus throwing out the money changers from the temple on the sabbath.

This is an early sign that commerce takes preference over religion not just today but also in the times of Jesus.

Remember this was not a Christian place of worship but a Jewish temple or synagogue.

Jesus seeing this was enraged and being the accepted son of God by some, threw them out of his father's house.

Since then, commerce is a black cloud to Christianity that hover overs important dates in the calendar, Christian religious festival, or even Christian way of life.

The presence has not moved or shift but instead stayed, evolved, and cashed out anytime there is money to made.

This does not seem to be such a problem in other issues with the Jewish festival of Hanukkah, also occurring in December, does not attract anywhere near the same commercial attention as Christmas and Easter.

For Muslim, wealth is not a factor in a place of worship with rich and poor people worshipping side by side.

There is little commercial attraction to tying Muslim religious holidays to the ramping up of commercial activities.

Christianity gets all the commercial attention.

This could be to do with the number of the world population claiming to be Christians, which could be anywhere up to a third of the world population claiming to be Christian either Catholic, Protestant or other breakaway sects of Christian who claim Jesus as their saviour.

CHAPTER 21

Christianity is the religion that has the most sects over any other religion in the world.

People have taken the teachings of Jesus and interpreted it their own way.

They take one aspect of it and a group of aspects and create their own sect based on their interpretation.

There is nothing wrong with this, but Christianity should be seen in its entirety and not just particular passage, texts, books, lessons, miracles, or teachings.

The whole picture better explains why certain decisions were made or why certain events went a certain way.

Why Jesus was crucified by his own people while a murderer was set free during the Jewish festival of Passover.

Why, who many would see as a good man, was sentenced to death in a torturous way, while a man who murdered was sent free.

Why Jesus own people turned against him and let another man get away with murder.

To many people reading this text today, it would seem unjust and a little bit crazy but this what happened.

The Jewish people where offered a choice, and they allowed Jesus to be executed.

The one interpretation one could get from this, is that Jesus was showing man the fallacy and limitation of their ways.

No matter who helped them and the reasons for helping them, they were doomed to repeat history and make decisions that would be their undoing.

Jesus was a lightning rod for their inadequacies and failures.

It is only after his death and resurrection, do people realise the errors of their way and hence the large Christian religion festivals of Easter and Christmas which are just Christian's realisation of their failures and the showing of guilt, remorse and appeasement through the use of gifting on the day Jesus was born.

The message that Jesus was sent to bring us was not lost but instead was borrowed by the commerce world to sell more of what we don't need in place of plenty of what we do need which is humility, humbleness and recognition of our ignorance and acknowledgment of our previous failures.

By celebrating Christian festivals so openly, we are giving off the impression that all is well and good in the world and the time of year that people are overtly nice to each other is pale and insignificant in comparison to the rest of the year when we show our true selves and can be backstabbing and vindictive to are fellow humans.

The adage, feast and famine are at play here and we are only good when we are expected to be good, and we are ourselves when nobody else is looking.

It has come to the gifting of presents of chocolate eggs at Easter, which meaning has nothing to with Christianity but to do with spring and pagan gods.

So, while everybody is watching we become a version of ourselves that we like but unfortunately that we cannot maintain.

To be good person all year round seems too many to be a difficult choose.

It is not a balancing act but a deliberate decision by many to be a lesser version of themselves than that which god would wish us to be.

Commerce has taken over from true worshipping and observance and the time of year that more Christians would visit their place of worship than the rest of year is not a time for reflection.

Instead to be seen by the neighbours, to meet old friends and catch up instead of observance of the true meaning of Christmas, that is the birth of innocence to save us from eternal damnation and the sin that eve bestowed on us from our birth.

Born of sin was supposed be washed away by baptism but instead it is being replaced by something far more dangerous and more hidden, that is our true selves and the combination of sins and failures that man has become in the time and since Jesus's birth.

The symbolism of the washing away our sins by the use of water, being that ninety percent of the human body is made from water, means that the ten percent that is left is either rotten or not the true creation that God bestowed onto us.

We are not a mirror of the god himself but have become something that was not originally envisioned and even thought about.

CHAPTER 22

Religion is associated with various empires that have been in existence but long gone where after military force started to wane or people started to shift their attention from their military leader to other matter.

All empires come into existence through military force and the conquest of foreign lands.

For an empire to be created and grow it need a large well-trained army.

A rag tag bunch or organised resistance is not going to become an empire.

It will become just that a collective or group of individuals who are looking to defend the lands against a foreign force.

The only organised group of fighters to come near creating an empire but not having the knowledge or understanding of an empire was the Viking.

The Vikings conquered and plundered foreign lands and many cities today were created as a result of Viking influence but the Vikings stopped short of the creation of an empire as there many reason was not of invasion and conquering of foreign lands but the plundering and steeling of treasure.

They returned to their stronghold with their blundered wealth to build up their influence, power and prestige.

It creates an empire you need god on your side, and your action are an extension of gods.

This was certainly the case for the Roman empire and more obvious the British empire.

The British empire is a good example of a power that was created and extended from their home bases in England to bring gods message and work to the world through first the conquering of foreign lands.

Next came the education of their people and then investment in their infrastructure which in time they would become a trading partner and asset to the empire.

Each country that the British conquered became part of their vast supply chain that provided raw material for their factories, goods for their stores and slaves and workers for their servants and large country houses.

The British had a template that they repeated throughout the world.

The template worked for hundreds of years until a time they had exhausted their available resources, or conquered lands saw a better alternative.

And a better alternative was independence but still being part of the trading block of the Commonwealth, which as a side remark is counter to Britain exit from Europe and the Common market.

But all this action was justified by gods work and the work of the King or Queen who was the head of their church.

The British saw it as their birth right to civilise the world and still see that today with much commerce being carried out through the English language.

But where did this belief come from and what is the justification for subjugating a people to their way of life and their rule of law.

The British colonise what was then known as Palestine and what we today call the middle east or the holy land or more directly the state of Israel.

The British controlled these lands and during various religious wars that occurred in the region, the British held this land.

CHAPTER 23

This land was holy for the three major religions as this is where Jesus, Moses and Mohammed grew up and taught their followers.

The fact that three significant religious people grew up so near together and would become their respective head of their religion has some significance for a person who controls the land from which these people came from.

It would be natural to think that this influenced the British psyche and belief system.

The fact that after the reformation period where the head of Monarchy became head of the church of England as opposed to the Pope, the king or Queen, been chosen as a representative of god and hold the territory of the holy land, this pretty much gave any Monarch a carte blanche to act whatever way they felt like.

What else did they need to own bar the original ten commandments or holy grail.

And it is from this just like the Romans adopting Christianity to support and extend their power base.

The British already being Christian in belief just needed the holy lands and the crusade proved their dedication to gods work and safeguarding holy sites and temples of which god is seen to have a presence or hand.

Today as the song Jerusalem rings around the fields of Glastonbury, just remember the real reason for the humming of this song, as the British people place and emphasis on their links to the holy land and the work that they carried out in god's name.

But were there no other reasons for this divine right to carrying out god's work.

During the Reformation period as England broke from the church in Rome, as the Pope would not allow King Henry the Eight a divorce.

For this break from Rome to be sold to the English people, England would need its own Rome and Canterbury which would become the seat of the church of England.

But this did not really have the international standings that Rome had at the time, but Jerusalem certainly did.

The occupying of Jerusalem and Palestine, the birthplace of Christianity would ensure that England, in religious terms would be held high in the world as they possess the birthplace of Jesus and from where Jesus followers came from and from where Jesus taught his followers.

To many it was a no brainer and to replace Rome with Jerusalem would be viewed by many as a step up not a step down or a step out to a different religion.

Once England held Jerusalem then all would be well, and this is where the term Roman Catholic comes from which British people like to use regularly to distinguish themselves from Christian in the holy land or Jerusalem from those with allegiance to the Pope in Rome.

Even though Rome was the capital of the Roman empire to many its significance was lost given that Christianity started in Palestine not Italy.

CHAPTER 24

The only place were ancient Christian were represented in Rome is the Colosseum from which they were killed either in bloody fight or burnt at the stake for not worshipping Roman gods but instead worshipping a man called Jesus who to the vast majority of Roman citizens nobody knew who he was or why anybody would want to follow him.

So, Rome nowadays is a strange place for the catholic church to have its headquarters, but these links are historical as opposed to relevant.

The Catholic church is an administration behemoth so being located in a capital city like Rome, the eternal city, is not the worse choose and in the days of the Roman empire, have the backing of the Caesar and Roman army was worth its own weight on gold.

The British were not the only empire to use religion to extend their reach and nowadays, it's the America army being sent into war torn regions in Africa and Asia that are there to bring democracy to these regions which is their religious beliefs through the back door.

No mention is made between how religious beliefs dictate how a country is administered.

Religion does play an important part in the evolution of the administration of a country.

Democracy is not the first choose of many Muslim countries and for many Muslim countries they normally band behind one figure, that either being a religious or military figure as opposed to the rule of democracy that has no real longevity and needs to be refreshed every few years.

Each democracy and their administration have a shelf life and the fact that you need a consensus and a majority to govern when most decision should be obvious is a major shortfall of democracy.

Doing the right thing should be the central theme to every administration and having and using an elaborate system such as democracy is too expensive, too time consuming and too wasteful for most Muslim countries.

Instead, they want a strong leader who is guided by religious doctrine and will do the right thing for his people each time not just when it suits him or when popularity is at stake. And for Muslims, having a leader who is morally incorruptible, astute, clever, and militarily aware is all the personal traits that they are looking for.

When they choose their next leader, it is these traits that they are looking for, not a person who is a good public speaker, looks well in a suit or knows everybody in the room but who's underlying make-up is unquestionable on their side.

Other empires that embraced religion as their guiding rule of God would be the Ottoman empire based in Modern day Türkiye.

The Ottomans believed in a sturdy base and that is why most of their wealthy and military might was focused on their capital city of Constantinople, or modern-day Istanbul.

Although they had the military power to extend beyond the borders that they created for themselves, they did not see it as their job to convert Christian race to people of the Muslim faith.

They were only interested in Muslim by birth and anybody else was either an enemy or not to be trusted.

Today we would call that keeping to your own people.

This contrasts with other empires who saw it as their obligation to convert a race of people from pagan god to Christianity.

For the Ottomans, this may have been a step to far as to convert a race to Islam seen a polluting the religion and race by introducing infidels who were impure into their religion and way of life and existence.

Muslim lands for the Muslim people and nobody else and this still rings true today with the implementation sharif law in some countries such as Afghanistan and the shunning of foreign people power and symbolism in exchange for a pure life of Islam.

Gods' way can only be achieved through military power and might and not through teachings of people, the way that Jesus envisioned that people would embrace his message and way of life.

CHAPTER 25

It seems that people were just not educated enough in the time of Jesus to understand the message he was bringing and it would take centuries for us to evolve as a people to truly understand what Jesus was trying to achieve and how the church continues to grow in order to meet the expectations that Jesus set down for us all those thousands of years ago.

We are now only finally catching up to where we belong.

But that is a decision as a race we made ourselves and that is a decision that needed to be made by ourselves and no other external or relatable force.

Empires have risen and fallen with or without the influence or religion, yet the institution of religion and their followers have lasted the ages.

With pagan gods being replaced by a single entity which is why it is so that an empire with all its influence and power cannot stand the test of time yet a set of beliefs and ideal last test after test and it seems it is reinvigorate or more focused as each new generation emerges.

CHAPTER 26

As a species it must be said that we are inherent and destined to be a good species.

It seems as we look back on history certain bad apples have emerged at key critical points in history and have influenced a whole generation to go in the wrong or bad direction.

Their misplaced ideals or interpretations have spawned generations of person with misaligned guidance of how they should live their lives.

Religion is a force for good as well as a force for evil and when a person of evil tendencies gets into a position of power and influence, they can do untold damage to a society and its people.

These people may start off with good intentions, but they realise to implement change and their vision in a quick manner they need to use threats, intimidation, coercion and bullying tactics to get what they want.

Change, in a society, general happens slowly and it must be the will of the people to want change to happen not just what a particular businessperson wants or a politician under the influence of a lobbying group wants.

Religion is not necessarily the agent of change but the teachings that will allow people to realise their god given potential.

Everything else is what we fall short off and just an excuse to substitute something else into our lives that we do not need or will just do us harm.

Many books have been written in the genre of self-help will try to empower us to change our lives which have been going in a certain direction, to make us stop, think, look around and realise were we are and where we are going.

By making a few simple changes to our lives our lives will become enriched with a new sense of purpose and desire, which is getting our mojo back.

Libraries are filled with these types of books and why they do help people it should be noted that this is nothing new.

The Bible and the Old and New Testament are exactly what this is about and more.

These books explain why people make certain decisions and why others make different decision based on the same facts and information.

RELEGATION OF RELIGION

In modern context, Moses ten commandments were one way God tried to get people back on the straight and narrow and away from temptations and associated sins.

People could either be good or bad based on the decisions that they made not by the collective decisions of other persons.

They were given this choice and as we know this new power given by God was short lived and people very quickly turned their back on this new power and decided that they did not need God in their lives and instead chose a different path.

A path where they could do what the liked with little consequences.

It is obvious looking back that these persons were not mature enough or developed enough for this new power and they reverted to their animal instinct.

There emotional intelligence was very low, their expectation of life and from life was even lower and they saw the world not as a canvas with which they could paint their lives using gods ingredients but instead a place to take and take what they want for their own consumption and satisfaction with little regard for anybody else but their own happiness.

That is a world full of selfish people fascinated with plundering all aspects of the planet resources to the full extent possible to ensure a steady stream of profit, performance, and enjoyment or as they see happiness.

A very one-dimensional view of the world.

Not much depth and breadth to this view of the world.

And this demonstrates to us the current limitations of mankind to move beyond the immediacy of every situation to a space or time where happiness and reward may look different and can only be experienced when we as human behave and act in a different manner to the current state of existence that we live in.

That means we look deeper into a situation and see how through our actions and interest we can make the world that we inhabit a more cohesive and rewarding place to live in.

Not just that through wealth creation but were we create happiness, people working and living in jobs and cities were they don't feel alienated or treated like outsiders, were people do not even know their neighbours, where addiction to harmful substances increases and where people give an outward impression that they are happy but in reality internally they are empty vessels and shells with nothing to give back to society and the only trace of their existence is in their workplace and nowhere else.

They have not made a dent in the universe or left a footprint of their existence but have gone through life first doing what their parents want them to do, then what their friends are doing, then societal norms and then what ever keeps their partner happy to keep their personal relationship together because they have a mortgage and car loan together and if they split up then they will be in a financial hell from which it may take years to recover and this would definitely effect their happiness level.

People these days are just sheep, following what is expected from them or what they think will make them happy.

Very few people have the freedom of thought to break this trend and cycle to live the way they want to live if there was no societal norms or peer pressure did not exist or if bullying was not around.

They fear breaking the norm because they do not know what kind of person they could potentially become and for them, and for society and for politicians and the business world this is dangerous, and this type of person could affect sales of products and services.

If people realised, they did not need all the products and service that advertising says we need to be happy, then a lot of companies could go out of business and a lot of people could lose money.

CHAPTER 27

Society is geared in such a way these days to the mass acceptance of consumerisation.

And for much consumerisation it is here to stay whether we like it or not.

And the most important aspect of consumerisation is that we accept the advertising, the sales pitch, and the marketing that we see and hear every day and get caught up in and brought along with this vision of mass consumerisation.

Mass consumerisation has gone too far and now more than ever people have been led astray by these marketing companies to lead a life that is hollow, wasteful, or fruitless.

There is no meaning to a lot of people's lives, and many people know that.

They are in jobs they hate and the only think that makes them happy is their pay check that they can spend on things they don't need instead of taking a look in the mirror and have a long and good think about themselves and asking some searching question if they are really happy and if they are doing the job that will make them happy or like most people, it is just a pay check.

And this is the power of consumerisation. It allows us to think that we are happy once we sign up to their false beliefs and promises and catchy jingles and phrase and all is good and funny in the world of shopping and spending money.

People have forgotten the true meaning of the gift of life and that life is a constant journey and re-evaluation of where we are at any given time and that we never reach a final destination but need to ensure that we are a positive force in the society that we live and not a negative force or worse still a force of destruction that so many businesses seem to be this day.

Who is going benefit from high profits and even higher prices is only confined to a small part of society, which being large institutional shareholders that manage people's pension and people rich enough to buy shares in the first place.

Most people do not have large share portfolio from which they earn dividends.

Most people do not know much about shares and the stock exchange and instead have learnt from the fiscal crisis of 2008 that there are more fools that join the stock market than that leave the stock market.

So, to many it looks like all the time, energy and resources that has been invested in the main organised religion has been in vain and we have not learnt any of the valuable lessons that they can tutor the average person.

To many the bible is a set of beliefs and teaching for somebody else, maybe the person on the bus or the man on the plane, but for them the Bible is something they prefer to keep at arm's length as to open and read the Bible will only quickly draw people to their own shortcomings and failures.

The bible holds a mirror up to each and every person from which they can gauge their own lives activities and benchmark themselves against other persons who arrived with a message but that has either been lost or distorted in the haze of modern day life and existence.

So even after thousands of years Christianity has been around it is still a reminder to people of their homework that they forgot to do and that needs to be done before they can move on.

Before they can evolve as an individual or better themselves for their lives and the lives of people around them. So, what is the next step for religion for it to keep its relevancy. This is an old argument that somehow religion must change or evolve to stay relevant.

The reality is that we as an individual must evolve or educate ourselves to see its place in the world and where we can be place in the world.

The rules have not changed, and the same lessons a thousand years old are even more relevant than they ever have been.

Their stories and teaching are structure in such a way that any person who picks up the bible can draw some level of understanding from it that will enrich their lives without the need to buy something expensive or go somewhere new.

So, we are destined to repeat the same mistakes, is a continuous loop of creation and destruction, something that we seem unable to break out of or worse still unwilling to break out of its endless cycle.

CHAPTER 28

It would be difficult to draft a book on the three major religions without drawing the obvious association between Islam and terrorism.

In the last three decades we have seen the invasion of Muslim countries such as Afghanistan by the Soviet Union in the 80's, the invasion of Iraq in the 90's and 2000's and the destruction of Palestine and Gaza currently and ongoing for many decades.

Where Muslim countries have been invaded you have seen an increase in terrorism activities and destabilisation in the region sows long term hatred of the foreign invading power.

This hatred turns quickly in to groups of individual banding together and form terrorism cells, all in the name of Allah, their Muslim god.

The holy Muslim book of the Koran has been interpreted, just like reading your tarot card and interpreting some upcoming event, which supported their belief that these infidels must be punished for invading their country.

The U.N. charter allow for countries to defend themselves against foreign power and in times of war do what they must for a country to defend its people.

Guerrilla war has been around for centuries and proven successful by the Americans against the British which resulted in Britain losing a big part of their empire.

So, although terrorism is a war and not a clean war at that which happens on a defined battlefield against known and labelled enemies, the war of terrorism is just that.

It is still a war and a war that is justified both legal and morally.

These are persons who are fighting a foreign oppressor who invaded their homeland.

As a person who has grown up in the West all my life, this might sound crazy especially when moving around cities both at home and abroad, but the facts and legislation speak for themselves.

This is no different to IRA prisoners in the maze prison in Belfast wanting political status as their fight was justified in their eyes and eventually led to an agreement which allowed them to be freed from prison.

As a result, they were defined as political prisoners as this would be the only way that they could be release from prison.

Parole or on license would not cut it for these IRA prisoners, so in some backroom in Stormont, a deal was made to allow convicted terrorist to not have to finish their sentence but instead leave prison after a respectable portion of their sentence had been completed and vow not to be convicted of another terrorism offense.

They were in effective given a free passage, an amnesty to leave prison.

Now this seems crazy, but this is what happen.

The people planning bombing campaigns in Northern Ireland and mainland Britain, killing, and maiming people, destroying lives and families and now they have been given what was called early release.

Their campaign was based on the vision of a united island where north and south of this island would be joined as one political administration.

The creation of Northern Ireland was not based on religion, even though planted persons were of the Protestant religion which eventually formed the breakaway part of the island called Northern Ireland.

The theory was that the planting of Protestant people would in turn breed out the Catholics within a region.

The bottom line is that Protestant family have far fewer children then Catholic families, to the ratio of four of five to one, that is for every one Protestant child that is born their four Catholic children born.

And this trend continued over the centuries up until the end of the last century. The Big Irish catholic families are not so present today, but this is not a religious decision but an economic decision.

CHAPTER 29

It is more likely that the reason for plantation was that foreign landowners would bring economic prosperity to the land by its better management for agriculture and crop management.

Before the creation of the landlord system within Ireland, natives all owned small plots of land which the tilled and managed but yields were low as the education and knowledge did not exist for how to get the most from the land.

The British realised that these lands needed to be better managed and so persons willing to migrate to another land were given the promise of land ownership.

For most landowners this was a second or third estate, with their primary estate being back in England. They farmed the land and agriculture yield went up. Locals were employed to farm the land and economic prosperity went up.

Infrastructure in the country was improved, and the general wellbeing went up.

It was not till the potato famine in the 1840's did modern rebellion come more to the fore and the need to remove the British from the Island of Ireland really begin.

So, when all was going well people were happy and content with their way of life but as soon as economic issues arose the need for independence increased and it is from these seeds that the modern IRA was born.

As the British left the southern part of the country in the 1920's, partition was created to protect the mainly and majority protestant people in the north who were alleged to their king not to the government in Dublin.

To the Protestant in the north, Northern Ireland was their home not mainland England and they swore allegiance to their king to stay.

So, this created tension in every sense of the world, a powder keg ready to go off and it was the modern-day bloody Sunday were this all kicked off.

Up until this point Catholics had to contend with a gamed system that is a system that supported Protestants and hindered Catholics.

Catholics had to deal with being second class citizens in their own land and not country. They saw Northern Ireland as their home and their allegiance was to Dublin not London. So, what we had was a stale mate with no one side willing to back down.

The issue was completely missed here. Both Protestant and Catholics were of the Christian religion and followers of Christ and if they dealt with their problems more maturely then there would not have been problems so great that they could not manage.

This may seem simple and for a southerner I would be told were to go if this suggestion were put forward, but nobody should or can be a follower of Christ yet lead such opposing lives.

Allegiance to Dublin or London, Canterbury or Rome does not make much difference when your faith and beliefs come from the same book.

So, what was the problems that could not be solved that led to years of troubles that it took a foreign superpower to bring all actors to the negotiation table and hammer out an agreement.

Both sides would not yield to the other sides demands. They would block each other's suggestions because this is how their society had operated.

People were given jobs and housing and government aid based on their religion not on their needs or their economic status.

When it came to the negotiation table this was not lost on either side and when it came to cooperating with each other and compromise, either side was not willing to yield an inch.

This is why external actor, and neutral parties had to be present at the negotiation table to ensure talks did not descend into the farcical and ridiculous but stayed relevant to the facts at play and the people's lives they were trying to protect.

During this process both sides realised they had the same fears, problems and anxieties and realised that they were not particularly different.

They realised maybe that this had something to do with their faith and the origin of that faith.

They had attended schools, and college throughout their lives based on their faith and not of their economic status per see.

The major dividing factor for both sides was their faith and not their economic status which is so often the case in most modern societies.

RELEGATION OF RELIGION

Both were following or at least labelled by every other organisation by their religion and nothing else.

It was Catholics fighting Protestant, not Irish fighting British, or English or Welsh or Scottish, no Catholics fighting Protestant.

To stand in Belfast and pick out a Protestant person or a Catholic person is difficult if not impossible yet the only dividing factor for these two groups of people is a book, the Bible.

A book that is the most sold book in human history, the most common book, a copy found in most hotel rooms, in people's homes and in libraries.

Now you may say that I am trivialising the situation, and I may say that you are over complicating the situation, but the reality is the situation is not that complicated and does not need to be that complicated.

It is us that has made a simple situation complicated by simply not understanding each other and realising that each person goes through different stages and we are allowed to change our beliefs, arguments and understanding as we grow old, become more educated or become more empathetic.

This is just the cycle of human existence and to cling onto old thinking and values is not doing ourselves justice and not really following the teachings of Christ.

We are at every turn selling ourselves short and not evolving as the environment and world around us changes.

Life is there to be enjoyed not endured and it is not that we need to go around helping people but just simply understanding people and understanding where they are coming from and what their present-day fears and anxieties are.

Because we cannot call ourselves Catholics or Protestants or Christian if we cannot get these basics right.

So, it is not that we need to hit a big reset button and go let's start again, no we just need to live and learn and improve and evolve into a better version of ourselves and this is really the message of the Bible.

Not to sow seeds of discontent and division but to live a life worth living and with that a life that will positively affect on all around us because as we improve so should those around us improve for the better.

CHAPTER 30

There is no doubt that there is an extricable link between Islam and terrorism and as we earlier explained some of this terrorism was born from the invasion of Muslim faith country such as Afghanistan and Iraq.

However not all terrorism can be solely attributed to invasion, and the religion of Islam is going through the same growing pains that Christianity went through in the last century.

Islam is a new newer, per see, religion of the three major religions by centuries and it could be said that the prophet Mohammed sees the shortcomings or failings of the message of Jesus, and this gave rise to the religion of Islam just like the short sightedness of Judaism gave rise to begin of Christianity.

These three major religions, even though they have had massive falling outs with each other over the centuries could be seen to be related but distinct with in areas that they inhabit.

All three major religions came about by one man trying to lead his people to a better direction.

The prophet Mohammed was about passing his teachings and message through the book of the Koran, while Jesus was more firsthand about his teaching were the message of Judaism and of Moses was about stories and teachings passed down through the generations.

These three major religions have had all remarkably similar teachings however the populations and basis that they stand for are quite different.

The cultures and countries that they are found in are vastly different and how each religion interprets the teachings of their prophet is hugely different.

And it is these differences that give rise to tension, arguments, and wars within the region.

Each persons of these religions have had serious communication or miscommunication with each other, and this is only exacerbated in the information age where it seems more misinformation than information exists on the internet and people are very easy to react to offensive posts, articles and even books on topics they know will cause turmoil and strive to a religion.

Some news media outlets seem only to exist to cause tension between these religions, and their existence must be questioned and verified.

Most people do not watch the news or even read the news these days as they do not know what to believe even if this news comes from a verified sources or is a state media official new outlet.

RELEGATION OF RELIGION

There is some much-represented interest groups and lobby interests that goes on for an organisation to get their side of the story out there at the expense of truth and civil obedience.

It is from this cesspool of inaccuracy and false reporting that grass root terrorist is born.

And this is how people are seeing the religion of Islam as it is seen as a religion of violence and terrorism as opposed to it true reason of peace, prosperity but more importantly empathy for your fellow man and been given the space to understand other people from different backgrounds.

Islam is the more open of the three major religions, but you would never think that as to the outside world Muslim people only want to live in countries were one hundred percentage of the population is Muslim.

This could not be further from the truth given that the religion is more modern than either Christianity or Judaism, both of which are international in their presence.

CHAPTER 31

It would be difficult for any religion to have a majority over any country in the world. The fact the Muslim world is centred in the middle east, just like Christianity and Judaism, is the fact that this religion stands for a different segment of the population, quite different to Christians and Jews.

Both these religions do not exist to take over the world or to control world governments, but instead to stand for the interests of their followers.

Much press has been given to Zionism and the Roman Catholic church and the power and influence that they have over world affairs.

If doing the right thing and living a life that is rewarding without hindering or hurting your fellow man, then this is the message that each of these religions brings to the world.

Most people may have an opinion on a different race or religion long before they have even met a person of that race or religion.

And these opinions are baseless and worthless but somehow, they take over people consciousness and understanding and belief system to the detriment of their view of the world.

It is only through travelling and experiencing these cultures do we understand the similar message and way of life that these religions exhibit and in some small way the world is a better place for this understanding and acceptance.

So, ignorance is bliss and acceptance has its limitations.

The growing pains that Islam is going through is like the Christian crusades and the Jewish people exodus from Egypt to the promised land.

Even as the Jewish people left in flight from Egypt through the Red sea and into modern day Israel, they did not create a country or put a stamp on the area that they inhabited and it was two centuries later after a world war and genocide, did the Jewish people realised the need to create a sovereign state to protect their people.

The city of Jerusalem did exist, but its close connection with the Jewish people was not known or just simply ignored.

Judaism is much older than Christianity and was terribly slow to this understanding, the Vatican in Rome is centuries old and is a fortified state with its own sovereignty.

RELEGATION OF RELIGION

Christianity, earlier persecuted by the Romans, now made their former enemies' capital their new home.

The Roman empire went onto ditch their own pagan gods for Christianity.

The only thing I can say is what a sell.

This is some turn around for a religion which goes onto to become the largest religion by population in the world today.

For the Muslim world, they also created strong holds and fortifications, whether it is the Ottoman empires capital of Constantinople or modern-day Saudi Arabia, which heavily invests on defence, the homeland of Mohammed and where each Muslim person prays to everyday, that is Mecca.

It is only in more recent times that the Jewish people realise the need to defend their people, even more so as god's chosen people and the birth of the Israeli state, predominantly sponsored by the United Nations, still had a lot of work to do to safeguard Israel from its Muslim neighbours.

Israel unfortunately has a lot of neighbours and not just one or two neighbours that they need to get on with.

Israel has a delicate balancing act managing the holy land and epicentre of the three major religions but at the same time managing is history and its future.

So why did it take so long for Jewish people to realise the need for fortification and defences and a homeland.

Being god's chosen people meant in effect that they were not tied down to any one geographical region in the world.

The land that is modern day Israel is more of symbolism and sentiment than being their chosen homeland.

If any area would be their homeland, it would be the Sinai Peninsula and Mount Sinai were Moses went up the mountain and wrote down the ten commandments.

This area is now located in Egypt and the fact the book of exodus, from the Old Testament is about the Jewish flight from Egypt and the miracle of the partition of the red sea means that the Jewish people could never see Egypt and their homeland again.

The next best area is the area called Palestine which already had a nomadic people and race present.

The Jewish people would have to share this land with other tribes.

For many years this was accepted and understood and did not seem to be a problem which tribes often trading wares with each other.

This existence occurred formed many centuries either as a province of Rome, a British colony, or part of the Ottoman empire the Jewish people were always subjugated to outside influence.

CHAPTER 32

Only when Hitler introduced the final solution for the Jewish people living in Europe did the need for an established state for Jewish people become paramount.

The German people losing a world war and finances in the 1929 wall street crash, needed a literal escape goat and no better people than a stateless people such as the Jewish race.

Hitler did not try to exterminate Christians or Muslims but instead what he saw as a race without a home.

If the state of Israel did exist in the 1940's it is unlikely that the same numbers would have been exterminated in the gas chambers of the concentration camps found in Poland.

The Jewish people, gods people were being eradicated in favour of sameness.

Hitler was there to create millions of clones of himself and unwillingly to accepted anything other than his beliefs and understanding of the world.

Hitler believed that the Aryan race, was the strongest races around and therefore must have been created by a god.

The fact that the Jewish people did not have their own country but instead were the richer segment of the population, a nation of shop keepers, meant that they were week and inferior to the German race.

This required great imagination on the part of the German race to believe this as the reality is that the lands of Germany were conquered by many empires since Hitler and at no stage was their even an inkling that this population would go on to believe that they were God like in anyway.

What Hitler did was brainwash a nation into his way of think and the best people at brainwashing are the people who are unstable themselves.

They have convinced themselves either through a traumatic event, such as being mustarded gas in a world was, which is what happened to Hitler, sexual abuse, abandonment by a parental guardian or another traumatic event in their lives which sows the seeds for brainwashing and the level of destruction that Hitler brought to the world by his arrival.

Hitler drew indelible lines on race, religion and creed which still exist today.

Prior to the second world war, most of the European royal family were descendants of Queen Victoria and her emphasis was on unity as opposed to division.

Religion was a belief not a divisive factor for her.

However, Hitler's arrival changed the landscape for ever and today which still have the battle lines drawn based on race, religion, and belief.

CHAPTER 33

As I draft this book, further destabilisation is happening in the Middle East with Iran and Israel exchanging missiles knocking out key pieces of infrastructure in each other's countries.

This ongoing conflict is not necessarily about religion but about power in the middle east and Israel standing up for its people and its sovereign territory.

Iran feels it is necessary to have nuclear weapons as this will mean instant respect from western alliances.

With help from Russia, Iran has slowly built up its nuclear programme.

There is no doubt that this programme is deliberately being slowed down by external influences such as the Stuxnet computer programme that caused Iran's centrifuges to exploded but also by the Iranian regime as the slow the upward percentage climb to 100% uranium enrichment refinement to some western powers is more acceptable as they are not in a rush to develop and use a nuclear bomb.

But just like nuclear north Korea, it is an important bargaining chip at the negotiation table.

The only Muslim state to be nuclear ready is Pakistan but this is a direct response to nuclear India as its neighbour.

Different religions and cultures even as neighbours, seems to always bring tension and some instances of war.

If your neighbour is militarily or economically stronger than you are, it is inevitable that your neighbour will try to enforce their influence on you, and this is no more evident than in Ireland whose neighbour occupied our lands for over eight hundred years.

So much so that their culture became a central part of modern-day Ireland.

When neighbours are of equal militarily and economic standing and have similar cultures then they will form alliances either economically such as the EU or militarily such as NATO.

So why do we need to be the same to agree on anything and what divisive factor does religion play on diplomatic relationships.

The question can only be answered by looking at human evolution and psyche.

Humans hunted and gathered based on similar needs.

There was no question about beliefs but instead who had the better weapons won as they were able to forage and hunt more game than their rival.

At this early evolutionary stage, military capacity might be the most key factor.

As the human spirit developed beyond subsistence existence to something more akin to today, various people created beliefs or found beliefs based on their environment, such as pagan gods.

Their existence could be justified by the presence in people's everyday lives such as the sun, moon, star, seas, and air. This was common amongst all human groups around the world even if not connected in any way such as trade or movement of people.

From these groups of people who normally ruled by consensus or majority rule, it is this change that brought about modern-day conflict both in religion and politics.

Each group found that to evolve to their next stage of existence, they needed to appoint a leader who would guide them based on their vision as opposed to the vision of the group or what the consensus or majority view was.

And why did this change come about, what was wrong with having their pagan representation of gods and consensus of a group of people.

The change came about when people felt that their pagan gods were communicating with them and sending them messages and advises on what to do in certain situations such as famine, war, or other forms of conflicts.

There gods were given places of worship and in some instances, sacrifices were made to a particular god to prevent or end a particular situation.

These gods were seen to have lofty expectations and elaborate, and expensive places of worship were built for them.

Over the years as people got more and more desperate, these places took more and more centre stage in people's lives to the expensive of their normal jobs or lives as the gods were seen to control, everything and all man could do was appease them.

No research or learning was placed on the science or agriculture which they had previously mastered.

RELEGATION OF RELIGION

Some races, experts in the movement of the sun and star and created the modern-day calendar based on this movement, knew when the best time was to sow and harvest crops to achieve a plentiful bounty.

But when their pagan god took over the running of a people based on the need to have an appointed leader who used the pagan gods to hold onto power and control the people that he or she was meant to govern, then the wheels really came off the wagon.

It was all about holding onto power as opposed to guiding people.

These appointed leaders now knew what it felt like to be almost God like and having people do what you wanted them to do based on how you were seen and perceived as opposed to the results that you were trying to achieve.

So is this about greed and corruption and nothing else.

How religion and God took centre stage to that of a maternal or mother figure such as mother nature which would seem to make more sense and logically follow the development of man from an agriculture-based economy which most economies started out to and services led economy which many developed countries have developed into with debt making up the trade imbalance.

This seems to be the answer, that for many years religion was used as a tool of blackmail for many leaders to get people to do what they wanted to do and many times what they wanted to do was illegal, immoral or just downright evil.

Yet this is the setup that we have today but instead of religion being the battering ram that we have, instead we have the tools of bullying, coercion, black mailing, spying and other nasty tricks which is the direct outcome of the use of religion for political and economic gain.

The roots of these immoral practises can be traced to when groups decided by consensus, which is a pure form of democracy, for the need to appoint a leader to guide a people in times when it was seen that a united vision for the future was required, which in reality already existed.

People were hood winked into creating an administration when none was needed in the first place.

This form administration went onto become government using various forms of political mechanism such as democracy, communism or socialism which gave us our present-day problems.

One person's vision or one governments vision or one parties vision or one assemblies vision is just that, as much as it tries to say that it is a direct representation of the view or opinion of the people, in reality it is most likely disjointed and far removed from what the people want and this is because something was created that did not need to exist in the first place.

The elevation of one person from being a normal everyday person to a leader had far further ramifications down the line and this can be seen by many modern-day leaders trying to act normal as possible to be seen as one of the people as opposed to being the out right leader of a country.

Many world leaders now try to cultivate a common approach, easily accessible or a normal persona as they realise there need is less and less required and the need for these bloated administrations and government is less and less required as many repetitive tasks can be automated just what was done with the car industry, once a big employer but not most of the car assembly work is now done by robots.

CHAPTER 34

What does government have to do with the regulation of religion.

Because government has stolen religions thunder.

It has taken its view of the world and the way the world should be, a natural division between the natural and the supernatural and this has cause nothing but turmoil in the world.

Government has not solved any problem that man did not create so to try and act in an elevated or God like manner is distorted and a bit of a cod or lie.

Man has created a bigger problem than the one that it was trying to solve, which was trying to bridge the gap between the divine and mortal and man himself.

It is probably the reason why God has left man alone for so many centuries, because man is in no state to do what was asked or required of him but worse still took it upon himself to seek answers by trying to join the ranks of the divine.

Every religion existence is attributed to the existence that is supernatural, out of this world and powerful, and man tries to continuously to harness this power in the belief that this will solve all of man's problems.

If this is the case then God would have made man to this level of existence, but the reality is that the heavens was for the mortals, and the ground and land was for the immortals, and each was aware of the others existence.

Any interactions between both levels always caused conflicts and tension and it was the decision that these interactions should cease to exist and that man should be left to develop in his own way based on existing teachings and the environment which man inhabits and any further interaction will have man thinking that he is special and requires gods help and interaction so that man can join these mortals in heaven.

But this was never part of the original plan, and this seems like it was thought up by man himself as opposed to being part of gods overall plan for man and the universe.

It is from this thought process or belief that all the problems of today are masquerade as, such as greed were people are never happy with what they have but continuously seek more and more wealth, power or recognition in the hope that this will bring them happiness.

But the root of the problem is that man is staring at heaven as the eternal reward for this existence instead of looking around at themselves and trying to better the world and people around them and realising that this is their eternal reward and the reason for this existence.

The hopes and dreams are somebody else's and not their own and this needs to be in constant competition with those around them is the cause of endless strife and difficulty in the world today.

This unending cycle of greed and power is a misalignment between the heavens and earth and how man reinterpreted a message to suit his own agenda.

Man has gone beyond gods vision for him and has taken matters into his own hands and acted against gods best wishes.

That is why every decision that man has made since this division has resulted in catastrophic consequences for humankind and his descendants.

In every interaction where God has firsthand tried to help man, this only works in the short term but in the long term this interaction by God has lasting consequences for humankind.

Two thousand years after the Last Supper, Holy Communion is still the main stay of the Catholic mass.

That is, we are still looking for forgiveness from God for our sins and Jesus is our man on the ground who is helping us out.

Our beliefs have not change, in fact it has only got worse in the sense that immoral practises have increased throughout the centuries and our need for forgiveness can be simple be guaranteed by a confession box or mass attendance.

Even the legal world cannot interfere with the goings on of the confession box and any sins no matter how grave can be relayed to a priest in exchange for absolution.

This rinse repeat cycle of sin and forgiveness purely born from eve's original sin is a cycle that man seems unwilling to break or evolve from.

It is like an addiction that is a managed addiction and an agreement between the church and its followers in the sense that if you commit sin, you will be forgiven but only if you are a follower of this church and faith and nobody else's.

This rings true for most of the other religions and of the other religions such as Buddhism which is about reaching a higher level of consciousness within our bodies and our bodies only being vessels which the soul inhabits, sins can also the cleansed through daily rituals.

CHAPTER 35

So, what is the next step for Christianity if it is indeed stuck in this time warp and repetition cycle were lack of direction seems to be an issue and the need to always return to holy scriptures, be it the bible, Torah or Koran instead of taking the lessons from each holy book and applying to our daily lives without reservation.

The holy books are a prop which we can lean on in times where we are unsure of the direction we should go in.

But is this the true function and purposes of holy scriptures.

Are they just supposed to be reference books in which we can draw correlations between a disciple or prophet of God and our own lives or is there a deeper meaning and purpose to these holy books.

These holy books follow the events of a holy persons be it moses, Jesus or Mohammed and other lesser well know religious persons and the events surrounding their message from God and how we should live our lives the way god intended us to live them.

The reality is that this collection of short stories is a recount of the events of a prophet within a specific time limit in their lives.

It does not cover all their lives works and teachings, and in the case of Jesus only covers really the time leading up to his birth and the time leading up to his death.

For Muhammed, the text was written when Muhammed isolated himself with the rest of the world and had direct conversations or interactions with God.

For the torah and Jewish bible, although Moses is covered within its texts it is more about the troubles that the Jewish people experience and multiple events and response that Jewish people deal with.

We can draw correlations between the stories of these books and our own lives and the trials and tribulations that life throws at us is nothing modern but as sign of the times in the way we can read our horoscope and interpret and reinterpret what it says about our star sign and apply it.

Each of these books was not meant to be the start, middle and end of the definition of a religion but instead meant to kick start a debate of reinterpreting old facts to a new way of life.

But instead, what we got was people returning to these books repeatedly in the hope that hidden message will appear of some new great enlightenment will occur.

The three major religions and their holy books are the most read and analysed text in the history of humankind. Every word and sentence have been analysed for added meaning.

There text has be run through computer programs with various algorithms to try and find any other hidden meaning or text that we missed or did not see on the first, or second or n'th time of reading.

These books are an oasis in a dessert, which is a place of certainty in a world of a lot of uncertainty.

It is a safe space and a place we can return to time and time again, be it at a religious occasion, in our own readings or just in conversation with others, but the problem is these books are no longer challenging us even today when our own failings mount and the teachings resonate, the message is old but more importantly the message has failed to reached us and mankind is no better of as result of returning to these religious books time and time again.

If a religion is based on one man's teachings and texts and way of life and this man is no longer alive in a way that that we can physically interact on a day-to-day basis, then what can we do, does this person learning and teachings stop.

If we look at the three holy prophets of Moses, Jesus, and Mohammed as modern day soldiers, they were tasked with a job, they executed the job and left the area to move on while still influencing what was going on.

People may see this as overly simplistic, but which is the truth, God intrusted each prophet just like he entrusted Angels and other messengers of God with a job, role, or task.

For Moses it was to guide the Jewish people, gods own people out of Egypt and into the holy land.

For Jesus it was to absolve original sin which was preventing people from getting into heaven and for Muhammad it was to lead his people into a more purer and cleaner existence and way of life that was free from sin and all pretence of sin, a more moral existence.

Each tasked with a role that they executed and when completed and they ascended into heaven to return to their original state.

Their influence was to create a new direction and like leaders today their influence should be temporary with others coming to the fore, such as Christ disciples and taking over leadership and setting the direction.

RELEGATION OF RELIGION

This is what every Pope since Peter has done but this direction is limited based on the teaching of Jesus.

A reboot of the catholic church such as what we had during Vatican Two assembly of church leaders did change the way the church ran, but the message was still the same.

This self-imposed status or paralysis has given rise to spin of religions of Christianity, such as Protestant itself, Mormonism, latter-Day Saint, Born-Again Christians and so forth.

All these religions which do command many followers have been created as a direct result of inaction by the Catholic church.

The inability to move beyond its current teaching and interpretations to a religion that is more practical, relevant, up to date and recent.

Many followers of Christ are looking for a new religion and identity and are afraid to covert to this more modern religion for fear of upsetting god and his teachings.

These new or more recent religions focus mainly on one aspect of a number of aspects of Jesus and based their religion on that such as the baptism of Christ in the Jordan river by Saint John, or the last supper and the power of the eucharistic or the miracles that Jesus performed.

Most of the present-day religion are directly or indirectly based on the teaching of Jesus and his followers be it Catholic, Protestant church or any of the number of other churches founded by Christian leaders.

It was envisioned that all the diverse religions would reunite under the one banner if there was ever a second coming of Jesus Christ.

But if there was a second coming of Jesus, what would it look like and would we be able to recognise it in the modern day with so much noise and distractions going on in the world.

CHAPTER 36

Our days and world are artificial busy or made to look busy given the number of things that we can do in any one day and the limited hours of the day.

We have deluded ourselves into thinking that we are extremely busy all the time and that we have too much going on in our lives for anything else than ourselves and closer friends and partners.

Are inflated senses of importance being just that.

It is something that we have created ourselves and is baseless and unjustified.

We are not as busy or important as we think or make out to be. This is just in our head and is put there by ourselves to make us feel good about ourselves, so we do not feel that we are missing life and all that is available to us to experience in this world.

As such we do not allow ourselves time for anything else and certainly religion and teachings of holy people is not front and centre in our daily lives but more of a throwback to our childhood or family lives.

The religion that we were born into is just that.

Most people do not keep this religion or relationship with God in the same way that they did in the earlier parts of their lives.

It is the earlier part of lives that shape us and to leave this out or not maintain this important link with the past brings up obvious questions as to what direction our lives are going to go in and are we leaving behind aspects that we saw as important at one stage.

With this, the return of Jesus to us may be so missed that it may have already happened and we did not even notice it.

It did not even create a ripple never mind the landslide effect that it had the first time around.

Jesus' relevancy is no longer justified in most people's mind as we feel that we have done it all as we race to beyond the stars there is not much left to do as a species.

We have done it all and now it is time to experience the bountiful reward that is left to us by others, and other sacrifices to gives us a world with so much potential and available to us at the click of a mouse.

Religion has become a defining division force in the modern world today were previously it was political beliefs and followings or geographical location.

As the world becomes a smaller place with the advance of globalisation, religion and not race it coming to the fore as a divisive force.

Across the world as faith is lost in democracy and the people entrusted with safeguarding our future, more protest is coming onto the streets.

This is a battle that started out as the people or citizens of a country against the government and internal or police force within a country.

However, as these protests escalate, they become something different, and the battle lines becomes redrawn.

For failing governments and countries with low government support to deflect the attention away from their inability to exercise the duty of office they have been entrusted with; they created side plots.

That is internal terrorism threats, garnering support from the media and other deflectory ideas to stoke tensions within society not based on government anger but on division and conflict within various strands of a society.

This is what has happened in such countries such as Egypt between Cope Christians and the Muslim majority population.

In recent times Cope Christian's places of worship have been target by either been burnt down or its followers attacked.

In Egypt Cope Christians and Muslim have lived side by side for hundreds of years without any issue.

Since the overthrown of Egypt's long-standing dictator, a democratically elected government which the west promised Egypt, like so many other countries would occur one day, has not delivered the intended results or delivered upon the withheld dreams of Egyptian people.

Dream which its people have been waiting for for so long, and as a result the fledgling democracy has had an upward hill march to delivering any real tangible benefits or results which the leaders of the revolution promised.

RELEGATION OF RELIGION

After all the euphoria of overthrow and revolution dissipates and the real job of governing comes to the fore, the same problems exist for a dictatorship that exists for a democracy.

However, people's dreams have not gone away, and the government had to produce a way to deflect attention away from them onto another part of society who are defenceless and open to attack.

This approach is no different to attacks on Jews in Germany and the creation of ghetto followed by concentration camps.

In Egypt this manifests itself against a minority Christian church.

This unfortunately works only works for a brief time and eventually people realise their problems have not gone away but instead have gotten worse but instead their list of priorities has changed.

Instead of being angry with the government for not delivering their promises instead, they are angry with a religious sect in which the media has done an excellent job of stoking up tension based on false claims or inaccurate reporting.

This same tact or approach is use in America all too well were ballooning government debt, a failing democracy and greed, the various government departments and arms are employed to sow discord and division at the expenses of a every changing minority group.

If you are Muslim, black an undocumented immigrant, refugee or convicted criminal you are no doubt going to be targeted by the media.

But the biggest factor is no longer skin colour or economic demographics but instead religion.

CHAPTER 37

Religion still plays a major part in America life, and it was the religions following that got Rove Versus Wade Court case overturned and led to abortions being illegal at federal level.

Now each state had to legislate for abortion.

In other countries were religion and the running of a country were no longer the same apparatus but instead two distinct institutes, America has shown that religion is still front and centre for most of the population.

This ruling along with the lack of gun control has taken away from the media spotlight being placed on the government's debt ceiling and inability to cut its dependence of debt to manage the economics of a country.

It may be the case that there is a need for people in America to return to their religious roots as a way of cutting their dependence on consumerisation as a way of life and instead return to more Christian values.

Since commencement of this book a new Pope has been chosen from conclave and for the first time, the Pope is from the north America continent and from the USA.

The previous Pope, from south America, is a way of the Catholic church acknowledging the large religious based of the Americas and how their way of life influences political and economical policies of their respective country.

The Vatican is a sovereign country and has the same problems just like any other country. The election of our present pope, a way for the Catholic church to exude influence in a unique way, not just purely in a spiritual way.

A head of state combined with the head of church responsible for the spiritual needs of over one point four billion followers as well as being the boss and payroll expert for many hundreds of thousands of jobs either directly or indirectly is a far more potent prospect.

The largest single owner of property in the world, the Catholic church has been punching far below its weight for years.

A new Pope will instead remove misdirection and miscommunication by the media, foreign governments and international agencies and instead would be more front and centre just like Christians in north America who protest and march for their beliefs not just their rights.

It envisioned that as countries around the world start losing faith in their appointed political leaders who's only economic policy seems to be borrow and spends instead of more conservative economic policies which will yield lower economic forecasts but instead have economies more stable and consistent.

This Pope maybe the most economic centric pope that we have had for centuries with more focus on the economic environment leading to its followers have a better standard of living and therefore being happier Christians instead of followers who are rich benefactors, have everything but lack moral and spiritual guidance.

What we could be looking at is an internal revolution within the Catholic church that is filling in the gaps left by present day democracies.

This is something the Catholic church is good at, that is educating, feeding, and employing a society with limited returns but with plenty of human capital.

People are turning away from long workdays, high salaries, and soulless employers.

People are looking for more rewarding careers.

Presently we see many people retiring early to accept a part time role in a charity or NGO's, making use of their experience and contacts.

The next step would be people becoming more spiritual or more aware of their surroundings or environment.

This may mean taking up past times such as yoga or Pilates where they are given the space to clear their minds and allow other thoughts and ideas to inhabit their brain, brains locked for many years on the need to progress one's career or social ranking.

The rat race, property ladder or keeping up with the jones mentality has taken its toll on all western societies and developing economies as well as third world countries were citizens turn their back on their country in the hope of reaching the west and all the west promises to be from the magazines and television ads that they have seen.

RELEGATION OF RELIGION

There is no doubt a roll back or retrenchment of consciousness with people no longer wishing for what they thought would bring them happiness as they had thought in years gone by.

When they have achieved their career goals or aim, they feel empty.

They have been climbing for so longer that when they final summit the mountain, the rewards are no longer what they thought it would be.

This is where the Catholic church should or will step in to provide people with the spiritual nourishment that they crave for or want.

This would be in the form of a renewed bond or relationship with their church, deeper faith and a new perspective or understanding of the teaching of Christ.

The sect, Born Again Christians, take a similar approach to religion, were people who have strayed from the church are brought back into its fold and reborn again in the teachings of Christ.

This approach may be broadened by the Catholic church, which accepts that many people are baptised Christians, but may not have been inside a church for years and may not have attended or taken part in a religious ceremony in years also.

Bridging the gap between the baptised and the faithful is the job of the new Pope and the approach taken may not be of the prodigal son, or lost soul but of a person feeding an addiction, that is the need or desire to feel loved, appreciated and understood which is lacking from many societies, workplaces and areas of socialising for many people today.

What the Catholic church offers are place for all this to happen, and this invitation has been put out for thousands of years.

Those who have accepted this invitation have gone on to lead happy and rewarding lives as members of the church and full participants of the church.

Their lives are more balance with little or no focus on KPI's, profits or efficiency but instead on the happiness of their fellow man, women or child and ensuring that the love of Christ is spread amongst those whose hearts are open to this love.

Unfortunately, these modern days does not really allow us to love somebody that we have never physically met or had a direct conversation with.

Instead, what we are left with a definition of love as a shared experience with somebody who we see as a soul mate and our other half.

This definition is based on co-dependency and the need to be loved.

In most relationships this may only last months or years, but for the Catholic church this should be an experience that we have for all our life, and this is the simple message that Jesus brought us.

CHAPTER 38

It is us who have redefined the message of love much to the detriment of our own personal and work relationships.

For the Catholic church it is about refocusing the message that Jesus brought to us and making it relevant and applicable for the twenty first century.

Many people, societies and ethnic groups have lost their way in the modern age of instantaneous everything and people are now not given the time or a chance too slow down and take stock of where they are in their life before making any fundamental shifts or changes in their lives.

The present craze is for people to rush to their early retirement and then decide to do all the things in life that they wanted to do but could not because their career and job took priority over everything else.

This is simply crazy way of living your life.

Life is not perfect, and your life will never be a perfect picture of your potential, possibilities, and dreams.

But this is what people want; they want perfection in their lives at all cost.

At the expense of enjoying life day to day instead of drudging through a forty year work carer, that they most likely hate, saving for retirement without enjoying much of the benefits that their carer brings them of worse still, always being jealous of a friend, work colleague or school mate who seems always to be doing better than they are doing, always seems to have a nice car/house/partner than they do and that is always one step ahead of them.

Yet this is what some people's lives have become, a fixed term rate race with a defined finish lines for when their second life begins or when they can start enjoying life again.

Some people still associate a big salary with happiness.

But their happiness is based on how they are perceived by others as opposed to how they perceive themselves.

They are in constant turmoil with themselves, constantly question themselves if they can do better, to push themselves on so they can push themselves up the corporate ladder to a bigger office, more responsibilities a bigger team or a partner in a big firm which seems to be the tipping point for most corporate aligned professional.

Yet as we have seen burn out, bullying, suicide, addiction, depression, unhappiness are the side effects of this way of thinking.

Unfortunately for some people it is too late, and they descend into a downward spiral from which they do not return.

And it is the absence of anything fixed in their life which is the greatest destabilising effect that causes all these problems in people.

By a fixed point, a set of guiding principles, beliefs and morals that is absent from a person's life.

We are not talking about an organisations' code of ethics, civil law, or other set of societal laws that people are bound by but in a religious or spiritual context a set of laws that defined your relationship with God.

For a time, it was seen as cool to not believe in a god or be agnostic.

But the problem with this is these people could never win an argument that God did not exist and were always on the losing teams.

Now these same people accept that there is a super being or person who has or is more powerful than the average person and has power over life and death, the universe and other aspects of life and the universe.

The argument was becoming too difficult to maintain and therefore a compromise was devised that allowed people to not have to accept religion into their lives but at the same time they had to accept that there was something out there in the universe that was more powerful than most, that could not be explained, that probably was not visible to most people but also is an immovable force that they had to respect, accept and live with.

These same people could live their lives in sin for most part, without feeling the need for forgiveness or change their ways or have pangs of guilt because again they did not believe in a god and therefore gods laws were not their laws.

Yet this is just what happened to these same people.

RELEGATION OF RELIGION

As they got older, they realised the priorities of their youth was different from their priorities of their older years.

They may have be born into a religious house and went through all the religious milestones associated with their family's religion and in their late teens of early twenty's, saw that religion was uncool, not relevant for where they were at in their life and just for old people or people about to get married or die, but not for them, and they went on to drop out of all religious activities and leave the religious family or community that they had been a part of in order to enjoy all the sinful aspects of life without feeling the need to confess or feel guilty.

It is not until later in these same people lives does this turning their back on God and church really start to show its ugly face in the form of a life without meaning and purpose.

On the surface they may be successful people, may have good careers and families, a partner and so forth but when you start to peel back the layers on this person life like an onion you start to see the real picture of this person's life, the gaps, the sorrows, the guilt, the hurt, the jealousy, basically all the seven deadly sins wrapped into one person, a cesspit of sin that has not been absolved of guilt by any higher power or force.

These people are a danger to themselves and everybody else around them including their family as their mountain of sin and guilt is like an out-of-control juggernaut that is just looking for an excuse to land on somebody else's plate.

They are hoping for a life event to occur in which all this guilt can be passed onto somebody else, another person who would have to deal with all their misdeeds.

This could take the form of another person's misdeed in which they can blame a person for all their consequential problems.

This could be an abusive parent, teacher or other member of the community who did something unto wards a person and it is for this reason that this person's life has become a train wreck.

But this is just a cheap parlay trick, a distraction, a misdirection from where a person can escape their misery or guilt for a few hours, which is just long enough for them to reset their speedometer for the next week.

They are using other people to allay their guilt, and this is the direct result of the lack of modern-day spirituality, acceptance of a higher power than their own and belief in a god.

CHAPTER 39

In their minds, God and religion has been relegated to a non-priority or bottom priority in their lives.

The space and time in their lives that was for religious practise, praying and spiritual reflection has now become devoted for sinful activities and when this sinful activity takes its toll they look for deflationary mechanism or the blame game begins, looking for a person or event to blame their lack of direction in their lives on.

This way of thinking is not just confined to a small segment of the population but instead, to large sways of the population who because tune out with the church or religion that they were following and choose a life that way not accepted or in the ways of the church that they were once a part of.

The Catholic church has recognised and classified this and these segments of the population as the lost sheep who need to return to the fold and the ways of Christ.

But this is the wrong approach to adopt.

The other wrong approach to take would be to water down Christ's teachings to make them more palatable to the mainstream population.

Both approaches would not achieve the intended results and would do more harm than good to both parties.

The watering down of canon law, the bible and religious theology would be an insult for most faithful followers of Christ and like everything in life, if it is not hard to do then it is not worth doing in the first place.

Jesus' testing of the human spirit is just that and the eternal reward of entrance into heaven should not be accessible to everybody of even every willing body but exclusively for those who can walk in Jesus steps and come through more enlightened, more focused and a better person.

This is what Catholicism, and all religions want for the individual and human spirit and the best approach for way ward Christians is for them to recognise the absence of something in their life.

To come to the realisation that this absence in their lives is the absence in the belief of God and accepting god into their life, a presence that has never gone away or turned their back on them but instead was always there for them and waiting for them in the hope that realisation would occur sooner rather than later.

Once a person re accepts god into their life, then the pain and hurt that can be attributed to a sinful life will start to go away that they can start living their lives normally again, not in the shadow of guilt and hurt but in public, front and centre as proud and honest disciples of god willing to live by the laws that god set down for mankind, without question and reservation.

They will become a better version of themselves and will truly be able to live their lives to the full potential that was meant for them to live.

The hollowness, shallowness and emptiness of a sinful life have been filled in with something more tangible, present, and usable in the form of God in their day-to-day life and decision-making process.

They will start to make better decisions as a direct result of this acceptance as their moral compass has been reset and realigned coordinated with Jesus' teachings and gods' laws.

Once a person stays on the path of the moral and just, then their lives will become ever more enriched, and betterment will occur.

However, gods teaching is not alone, and they must also realise that bad and immoral practise have not gone away, it is that they are just not allowing them time to rest and stay within their lives.

They still need to look out for all the signs that this sinful activity creeping backing into their lives in a stealthy form or a different form to the last time they entertained this way ward activities.

CHAPTER 40

It would be impossible to draft a book about religion and its place in modern society without writing about the connection between the faith of Islam and Muslim terrorism.

It seems ever since that day in September 2001 all that we knew about the world suddenly changed overnight without anybody realising.

The repercussions and ramifications of the events of that day had far more reaching consequences than anybody could have imagined.

Since then, everything about travel, religions, economics, and people's way of life has changed and nobody is in any shape is the better of for it for the actions of that day.

It seems that many people's lives are frozen since that day and they have not been able to move beyond the actions of fundamental terrorist hell bent on destroying the lives of people they never ever meet, knew existed, or even understand how they lives were supposed intertwined that they need to commit such atrocities.

Yet this is the narrative that is been played out by the media, government agencies, and foreign relationship bodies, that well trained Muslim people planned and executed the events of 9/11.

Their leader was a member of the Saudi Arabian Royal family who became disenfranchised with their way of life so move to Afghanistan to former mujahedeen fighters who controlled Afghanistan who had enacted Shari law on the citizens of the country.

Ever since the withdrawal of Soviet Union troops from the country, no central government existed, and it was seen as ripe grounds for training camps which were well funded by the sale of opium to western countries.

This trade triangle consisted of the growth of poppy to be cultivated as heroin, smuggled and sold to western countries, which monies went to buy weapons to be used to train new generation of fighters.

These fighters would be then sent to western cities to commit various atrocities.

Yet up until the start of the new century, these attacks were confined and were not based on a religious context but more on foreign powers trying to control Afghanistan as it was the country that stop the Soviet Union's further expansion south and west wards.

Just like the state of Palestine, to have control over Afghanistan is a power statement to the rest of the world and a trump card for the other superpowers that I have what the Soviet Union could not have.

It may seem petty, but this is exactly how foreign politics work.

But the afghani people are not dumb and they know this.

Just like the withdrawal of U.S. troops at the start of this decade, and the withdrawal of British and French troops in previous century, it seems that Afghans title of graveyard of empires is fitting as every empire that has gone into Afghanistan to take over the country, did not leave as an empire.

This is true of the collapse of the Soviet Union shortly after its withdrawal, the slow decline of the British empire in the decades after it left Afghanistan, the loss of international position to America after its withdrawal from Afghanistan and the end of the French Republic in the years after its withdrawal.

So, Afghanistan is a country that any foreign power can control and as such the perfect place for terrorism to reign supreme but also an easy escape goat for western powers in the years after 9/11.

But are we not missing the fact that every country is entitle to self-govern and the fact that the power of the Taliban, with its roots in the mujahedeen, was all about defending its home land against a foreign invasion, which many modern countries today had to do at one stage or another.

All that these guerrilla groups were doing was using foreign purchased weapons with foreign money to train their own people to fight against a foreign enemy.

How did these people go from a self-appointed milia group to a world franchise terrorist group committing some of the worst terrorist events in human history.

Events which have left an indelible mark on people's memory.

The vast and overwhelming population of Afghanistan is Muslim with some people of Christian faith interspersed with the population.

The Taliban were blamed for the attack on the U.S.S Cole, underground bombing of the World Trade Centre car park, 9/11, Paris Bataclan attack and London's 7/7 attack as well as many other inspired or copycat attacks.

RELEGATION OF RELIGION

In the years since the withdrawal of the Soviet Union army from Afghanistan, the collapse of the Soviet Union, fall of Communism, and rise of the internet, the Taliban went from a well organised militia group to an international terrorism group.

Yet as we look through the Taliban files, we are unable to find when exactly this occurred.

There is no defining piece of evidence that tells any intelligence agency, ah yes it was because of this event/action/person that the Taliban was launched onto the international stage with the new agenda, resources, and capabilities to commit the events of 9/11.

Yet when we look at the names of the person on the fives planes of 9/11, the cock pit recordings, visa, bank transactions and other evidence, it all points back to person trained in Afghanistan by the Taliban who were sent to the U.S. to do initial exploratory groundwork, training and testing before the big day.

These persons who were not on any western intelligence agencies radar, but post 9/11 their names were even know to the public, rose from obscurity to become masterminds and executioners for thousands of innocent people.

The back story seemed to be very similar also just like Osama Bin Laden's story, from wealthy backgrounds, some spoilt child rebelling against their parent chosen way of life for them, who want something more from life that merely being wealth, living the western life with all its trappings.

Instead, they wanted to live in a cave, play with guns, kill people and all in the name of Allah.

Its seems that their western life was soulless, meaningless and did little for them, but they were worthy of something much bigger and better, in some way they wanted to make a dent in the universe at the expense of other people's lives and happiness.

For them, their eternal reward was the misery and pain of other people.

They were not interested in helping other people or making the world a better place for all the citizens of the world.

Instead, their happiness was solely based on the unhappiness of other people.

They were feeders of other people's misery.

The definition for this type of person is that they were sadistic people.

Sadistic people do not normal have any room for other people in their lives, never mind allowing God into their lives and accepting his teaching and the beliefs and following of his prophets and disciples.

If these people were true followers of Islam and followed all the teachings of the prophet Muhammed, it is very unlikely that they would even come remotely near becoming radicalised terrorist of Islam.

The religion of Islam does not have any tolerance for one group of people inflicted their beliefs or pain on another group of people.

It is just not the Muslim way, and it is in no way connected to the teaching found in the Koran.

In fact, what they are is false believers or the very evil that Muslim people should remove from their lives and be in no way connected to.

The Muslim faith believes in purity of the soul and individual.

That means it is the responsibility of each Muslim individual to purge themselves of evil thoughts, actions or deeds that go contra to the Muslim faith.

The Muslim pilgrim, the hajj is all about the process of purging oneself just like the stations of the cross is to Christians.

The Muslim faith, just like Christianity uses water to wash away or sins and impurity, the flagellation or punishing exercising such as walking in extreme heat as punishing the body for the actions or inactions that it performed.

All Muslims are required to perform the hajj once in their lives, normally a little older as it is accepted that people are only human, they will sin and sin again in their lives, yet they are given a chance to redeem themselves by allowing God into their lives.

It is unlikely that the anyone associated with the actions of 9/11 went straight to Mecca the next day to seek Allah's forgiveness if indeed the actions of 9/11 were done in his name.

Osama bin laden certainly did not go back to the country of his birthplace and to Mecca to seek Allah's forgiveness, the so-called mastermind of 9/11.

If he were a true Muslim and believer, he would never have turned his back on his family and left his home country to live with a domestic terrorism group based in Afghanistan.

This is not the teachings of the prophet Muhammed, and it runs against all that is Muslim.

RELEGATION OF RELIGION

This can only lead us to believe that they faith of Islam was used as a smoke screen for a far different purpose, and the fact that so many superpowers had passed through Afghanistan at some stage, was a way of muddling the water for all investigators and investigations post 9/11.

Afghanistan's history was shaped by foreign power and their access to technology left behind by a retreating Soviet Union army provided some of the hardware for committing such an act.

However, the ability for a foreign citizen to travel to another country such as the U.S., register for flight school, receive lessons, training, examination and pass even pre 9/11 was not an easy task to undertake.

Even if Osama Bin Laden used his network in Saudi Arabia, who were on very friendly terms with the Bush family, it was still no easy task to undertake.

To coordinate the mass hijacking of planes and reroute them to large, populated cities, without getting shot down, is also not an easy task to perform for a backwater terrorist group from Afghanistan.

The mastermind of 9/11 would have had to have had inside people or persons within the major agencies within the U.S.

The U.S. is a predominately Christian society, and bar the fact that most of their oil comes from Muslim countries in the middle east such as Iraq and Saudi Arabia, most U.S. citizens in the start of the century did not know much about the Muslim faith.

Although all events on that faithful day in September when the bodies of the deceased are forensically examined, their travel documents checked, family and friends and work colleagues statements taken and all leads thoroughly investigated, all points to a Islamic terrorist plot, conceived by the mastermind Osama bin laden in a cave in Afghanistan with little or no western backing, it is a hard truth to swallow.

Are we looking at some sort of cover up, conspiracy theory abound, is there or was there something deeper going on that spiralled out of control, the consequences that we are still dealing with to this day.

The only way is to examine the fact.

The Mujahedeen from which the Taliban directly grew from was directly supported by the office of the U.S. President during and after the invasion of Afghanistan by the Soviet Union.

This was yet another proxy war between the two superpowers who were afraid to go head on in a direct conflict between each other and instead fought their wars in other people's countries.

Other countries that they used in this context was Vietnam, Somali and off course Cuba.

The Mujahadeen was trained and armed by the CIA and received all their weapons from the U.S. army stores.

The spread of Communism was of paramount importance to the U.S., and its stopping was of national security to all cold war White House administrations.

When the Soviet Union left Afghanistan and drew down their troops, this newly armed militia was allowed to hold onto their arms and not though was given to a post war government or administration for Afghanistan.

So, what you had was the wild west, a lawless country in Asia, covering vast terrain, with little or no central administration.

The Soviet Union in their speedy overnight retreat from Afghanistan also left behind munitions and miliary hardware which would slow down their withdrawal.

This included tanks, guns, and RPGs to name just a few.

This proxy war ended but not though was given to taking the arms of the table.

To own a gun in Afghanistan was a basic requirement because everybody else had one therefore you needed one.

This was a major cultural shift in the space of a decade when the ownership of arms was low.

What you had now was a large mountainous country, sparsely populated, with no central government, were many citizens owned weapons and had been taught to use tanks and RPGs by foreign intelligence services.

Citizens were used to collaborating with foreign intelligence service and new the lingo and tactics that they used in the era of the cold war.

This no doubt sowed the seeds for further conflict and effectively kicked the can down the road for a new generation and new war to be resolved.

However, you also had a majority Muslim population with little or no internal civil wars based on religious terms but instead war lords controlling vast tracts of land using cold war armoury.

The Taliban was the military group that evolved from the remnants of this proxy war, and they wanted a country that was completely Muslim controlled.

They did not have any ambitions beyond their own borders, and their primary concern was about enforcing Shari laws on the citizens of the country.

Any western influence was not tolerated and the punishment for abuse of these laws was death.

Most citizens lived in fear of the Taliban and to get on with their lives, just obeyed the laws.

As this way of life was against all western culture and teachings this no doubt went against widespread belief.

And this was the way of life up until the point America invaded Afghanistan at the end of 2001 in response to the 9/11 attacks.

In the space of two months Afghanistan went to a back water country, living in the dark ages under a sort of military junta exercising a form of religious laws to the masterminds behind the greatest terrorist attack ever carried out in the world.

To say that this is stretching the imagination is an understatement but to print this can also to see as a betrayal or offense to all those people who died on that day.

The reality is over two decades on we are no wiser to the facts behind what happened on that day.

For any democracy who is founding principle is the truth then this looks like one hell of a cover up and everybody thinks it, but nobody is saying so.

This is why democracy is been seen as so week and unable to fulfil the promise that it sets out to achieve.

The biggest victim of 9/11 is democracy as we look around democracy is unable to solve the problems of the world.

So, if the afghanis and Taliban were not personally responsible for 9/11 then who was and what was their reasons for conducting the 9/11 attacks.

Religious fundamentalism was seen as the overwhelming reason that the media and investigators decided was the reasons for 9/11.

9/11 did start a new religious war and brough America's medalling in other countries affairs home to roost however 9/11 was not about the intelligence communities failing or leaders inactions, it was about how five planes could be hijacked and flowed into major buildings were thousands of people worked.

It was known in advance that a plot like this was possible, but it was deemed that adequate security was in place to deal with such possibility.

The hijackers would first have to get into America, which was not an easy task pre 9/11.

Then they had to be trained as pilots who could fly and understand a Boeing plane, which again is not an easy job.

This was because even though pilots who execute some orders that a hijacker who ask them to do for the sake of their passengers' lives, once the pilots knew what they were planning, there would be not logical to continuing with their orders.

Next, they would have to understand the planes telemetry and navigate the planes dead centre into these building while avoiding other equivalent size building nearby.

They would need to know and executing the best flight paths available, as well as having the desire and willingness to commit suicide and the murder of thousands of people.

These skills do not come naturally to most normal people, and this type of training would only be seen in military wings and more specifically special forces.

They would have all the skills, experience, knowledge, and intelligence as well as an Afghan back story to cover their tracks to execute such a plan.

It is general knowledge that the military budget of the U.S. went up by trillions post 9/11 with military contractors becoming overnight billionaires.

A new government department was set up called Homeland Security that was responsible for funnelling all security threats and resources into one office.

This name personalised the threats that existed for America in the world.

RELEGATION OF RELIGION

Billions and billions were spent by America on security and foreign wars which wasted money and lives and achieved extraordinarily little.

Afghanistan is back in the hands of the Taliban; Muslim terrorism is bigger than ever, and more is being spent on security which is further pushing countries into debt and defaulting on their loans.

What about the Taliban.

Did they not have any hand to play in the 9/11 attacks.

I would say the first the Taliban new about 9/11 is when the only black and white television in the village is turned on and the images of 9/11 were broadcasted back into Afghanistan.

They were the last people to think that they were on the hook for such an attack.

As an ally of America in times past against America's biggest enemy of any time, the Soviet Union, still using some of their weapons and trading using U.S. dollars while also supplying the west with its opium requirements, it was unconceivable to the Afghans had made it to the top of the list as America's most wanted terrorists.

Yet this is exactly how it panned out and within two months Muslim extremists, based in Afghanistan were singled out as the masterminds of 9/11.

And while the America's were at it, we might as well get rid of Saddam Hussein finally, as he was no longer listening to America leaders and was the captain of his own ship.

The scaremongering by Sadam by the invasion of Kuwait was another ploy by America to further militarise the Middle East in the attempt to secure their oil contracts.

To many it looks like the religion of Islam is being used as a cover story to execute political policy and further expand big business into areas of the world with lucrative returns.

The capitalistic country of America were business trumps politics; it seems that the use of war as a money-making machine is back in vogue which died a death after two sequential world wars of the previous centuries.

The cold war was a sort of compromise with the use of trained intelligent agents as opposed to soldiers carrying out the orders.

The limitation of this policy was shown, and now more highly trained and equipped soldiers were carrying out the orders of the politicians with the backing of big business.

There can be no doubt that the events of 9/11 were a contributing factor to the decisions made in and around what became the start of the fiscal crisis of 2008.

Short termism was now in vogue as people feared for their way of life.

People were looking and making their decisions based on the near term as opposed to the long-term policies which is the basis of all financial thinking.

The passing and repackaging of debt in a pass the parcel fashion resulted in the creation of a toxic banking environment in conjunction with distorted of biases news feeds and corrupt politics and bad business looking for an escape goat to blame.

That escape goat was not a single country, or race or ethnic group but instead the religion of Islam.

Just like in previous centuries Judaism and Christianity, founded in the middle east but did not spread much beyond the countries and territories where it was founded.

This religion was singled out as the new internation dumping ground for everything bad that the western world did but could not blame itself for creating dot com.

The pure religion that Islam was creating and living with was suddenly polluted with the toxicity that the west had created.

Islam has become the scapegoat for Christian and Jewish religion.

When looking at it in its entirety how can one religion be responsible for such a trail of destruction.

Yet this is exactly what the media and international organisations are telling the public.

A religion that is predominantly found in the Middle East is now all of a sudden responsible for all the problems of the west from wars, price increases, financial meltdown, social upheaval, mass migration to destabilising religions can now all be pinned of Islam.

Yet the spread of the new wave of unpopular revolt against a religion has happened at a far greater pace than the spread of the religion itself.

The rise of islamophobia has been in parallel with the rise of technology and the spread of the use of the internet and the number of devices now connected to the internet.

RELEGATION OF RELIGION

The increase in internet nodes, trans ocean cables, fibre connection has also been kin with the spread of Islamic terrorism groups pocketed in the most unlikely places in the world such as Oman and Kuwait.

Even though these countries are Muslim based societies, they were once stable countries not associated with supporting terrorism.

CHAPTER 41

The internet has become a sort of petri dish for all that is evil and perverse in the world and this media is converting general disdain for the way that some democracies elected officials are governing their countries, either by being incompetent, corrupt or just lining their own pockets any chance that they get.

This anger is manifesting itself on the internet at a faster rate than any protest or demonstration can be organised.

Organised protest which sometimes lead to riots against police force is still occurring on a greater and more frequent level than for any earlier generation or time in our history.

It seems these days many groups of people have a gripe against their government and the way it is ruled.

There is protest all sort of government decisions, policies, and approach to domestic and international events. All that many countries can do is deflect attention away from what protestors and protesting onto something more divisive or unifying depending on how you look at it and sadly this normally takes the form of Islamic terrorism.

Protests are occurring increasingly in destabilised or failed states around the world which governments love reminding their citizens of places they should not travel to, and reason they should not travel to such a region.

These places are made out to be active war zones, normally Muslim countries when in fact they are peaceful and quite without terrorist going around in four by four pickup truck tooting semi-automatic weapon while firing them in the air, like what we saw when Libya fell from Gaddafi's control and was taken over by western backed rebels.

Islam is just getting a bad rap and there is no international head of the religion, such as a Papal figure that would bring better public relations to the religion and remove many of the myths and false truths of the religion.

The reason for the religion of Islam not pushing or advocating for a central figure is because the religion of Islam is about your direct relationship with God and without the use of an intermediatory.

When you are reading the Koran, you are reading the words that God wants us to hear, know and understand.

You should not and do not need an intermediatory for you to teach, translate the words of the text for you to understand what god is asking for you to do.

This is a completely different approach to that, that the religion of Christianity takes which is about the stories of Jesus, sent by god to purge eve's original sin and from which the church of Christianity and its many different interpretations is about the constant and continuous teaching of its followers, which seem never seem to understand the lessons that Jesus is trying to teach us.

I do not know how many time I have heard the some passage of the bible being read, or the same letter of one of the disciples being read or the same reading from one of the bible being read, only for it to fall onto deaf ears.

Why are people going to their place of worship, listen to the same texts and readings and lessons of Jesus, only for them to going out the door again and forget all that they have heard and continue on with their lives in the exact same way without having learnt anything or worse still as if they had never been to church in the first place, in one ear and out the other.

It seems these same people become robotic in nature, go through the motion and forget all that they have learnt, yet when they hear people quoting passages from the bible to support their argument, giving some structure to their day or lives, these people are labelled as crackpots or nutters who are bible bashers or who have lost it.

Yet this is the exact same book that these people have based all their religious beliefs on for whole of their lives.

It is just not cool to be seen to be religious or even to have read the bible.

The sense of individuality has been lost because it is seen that Christian have not left the classroom and the only people that should be teaching about God are priest and vicars.

Anybody else should just stay quiet and listen to what the preacher is saying.

This is certainly the approach in Europe.

In America, there is a different approach taken, which is more based on community based religious programs and not just based on your relationship with God via a Priest, Vicar or Preacher.

The approach is about the inclusion of religion in all aspects of a person life not just on one day a week or one hour a week.

RELEGATION OF RELIGION

The inclusion of the bible and books of the Old and New Testament in people's lives, removes the stigma associated with the presence of religion and God in people's life.

It is not just about showing up once a week at church but practising what you are preaching.

You should no way be embarrassed about owning a copy of the bible, reading a copy of the bible in public or be able to recite your favourite passage, or text from the Bible.

The bible is a fixed reference point for many people's lives in America, a guiding light that many people refer to in time of difficulties.

One of the groups with the highest rate of ownership of a copy of the bible are prisoners.

That is people who are incarcerated for the rest of their life and their only salvation is God and the bible.

They are in prison for a reason, they have received their sentence, and just like Jesus who was trialled and executed, these prisoners are going through the same process, albeit two thousand years apart.

Prisoners recognised that the path to redemption is about the acceptance of Jesus and God in their lives.

It is not a question about being popular but about finally doing something for yourself, thinking about yourself first.

For the religion of Islam, which was text written down by Muhammad at the behest of God, to be distributed, word for word to followers of Muhammad.

This direct relationship with God is just that.

Although Muslim can be seen praying in large groups in mosque, the reality is most Muslims will choose to pray alone and in private as they feel that this is the best connection with God.

Prayers, occurring five times a day, based on the position of the sun and pointing to the holy city of Mecca, is about your own conversation with God.

There is no need for a mass show of obedience, as you would see in a place of worship but take the personal responsibility to keep your connection and relationship with God.

It is the responsibility of each Muslim to keep a constant state of cleanliness' and purity both physically and mentally.

A healthy and clean body will encourage a healthy and clean life, and it is only if you are clean and pure can you expect to have a direct relationship with God.

Otherwise, it is just window dressing or just putting on an act for everybody else except yourself.

For these people they lack the emotional dept to have any relationship, not even with themselves and therefore they will never have a true and honest relationship with God.

They are only fooling themselves and this act is just that.

A person who is more emotionally developed, aware of their surroundings and happy and love themselves will then be able to love and care for others.

These people are not worried about what other people think about them.

They are only worried about what they think about themselves.

They are happy in themselves and content in their lives.

They do not have the need to help others to help themselves.

People who go out of their way to help others, are hollow people and lack any such depth of personality and character.

Their existence can be measured by their need to help others.

These people do not have the energy or desire to sort out their own lives but take it upon themselves to sort out other people's lives to use as a sort of proxy for their own unhappiness.

If they can make other people happy through their action in their lives and inaction in their own lives, then they can be happy in some, albeit for a brief period.

Then they must do it all again the next day, helping somebody else for get back to the state of happiness in their own lives.

These types of people could never be true followers of Islam, as it is essential in Islam to help yourself first, as God would wish, before you go around helping others.

In Muslim country there is no were near the same level of charity in societies.

RELEGATION OF RELIGION

Although donation is a part of Islam, it is associated with religious festivals or exercises, a close association with the purging of one's sins, the betterment of the individual and the giving of monies of time for a specific and defined cause.

Donation should be for a specific task, job, or goal, not an open-ended invitation to get involved in a 'good cause' just so you can feel better about yourself.

There does exist a gap in progression or evolution between the religion of Islam and Christianity were the Pope is still playing the Shepard to his flock, the patriarchal head of the church, the all forgiving parent which in this modern times maybe a bit dated.

The problem seems to stem from the lack of ability of the Catholic church to push the teaching of hell and Satan as the eternal punishment for any Christian who betrays their faith and is dammed to hell for all of eternity.

Instead, the Catholic and Christian church takes the high road in that no problem is too great that it cannot be fixed, absolved, or forgiven.

The problem with this teaching a belief, is that evil or the act or carrying out bad deeds is not about the deed itself but the person who carries out the deed.

If you believe in God, then you must be able to believe in the division or life and the universe into good and evil.

That is people who are brought into life and the universe who are fundamental of a good standing.

That is to say that their moral compass is pointed in the right direction.

This is not to say that these say people are going to commit bad things or do wrong it is just that their default position when they doing something wrong is in the good setting which makes is easier for us to understand where absolution comes from or the concept that all sins can be forgiven.

However, for these same people to commit wrong they will be influenced by a group or set of people hell bent on causing destruction and ruining people's lives and property.

It is my belief and understanding that these same group of people are the perpetrators of evil acts and deeds in the universe.

They are pure evil, and they can only propagate through their evil acts.

They spread all their deadly vices of lying and deceit and manipulation throughout the universe through any media and means that they can get their hands on.

This is their goal, the battle of good versus evil has never been more front and centre or divisive in the history of man than the present day.

Earlier World Wars have been orchestrated by the same group of individuals such as World War One which was started by the assassination of a Duke which led to the deaths of millions of people around the world.

All the earlier wars combined did not come close to the number of people who died in World War One.

Yet when we look back at the event it is exceedingly difficult to justify this war.

All the heads of the various states were related to each other either by marriage or biologically for the reasons to prevent such wars occurring in the first place.

But even with all the deliberate acts that occurred, no doubt some people knew that such a war was bound to happen, we ended up with a war of unprecedented scale, a war were the machines and training of soldiers had not evolved beyond horseback riding and charging at the enemy and worse, trench war fare.

It was a war from a previous century.

Yet this war did happen, and it ended up with a fragmented continent with destroyed infrastructure.

At the end an armistice agreement, a stale mate where no side claimed victory was the outcome.

These same family members who only hours before were at bitter war with each other now agreed to put their differences aside.

This however was short lived, and Germany ended up being labelled the loser of the war and the cause of all the unwanted destruction.

There is no doubt that external actors must in some ways have been involved for these events to occur and sustain for more than four years.

These same evil people that we know exists in our society must be responsible for these events.

And this is repeated throughout history with many other wars, events occurring to upset the apple cart of peace and prosperity in our society.

There is no doubt that the Second World War was the sharpening of these same people's agenda, which is the war of good versus evil.

It takes a special kind of person, peoples, or race to want to eradicate another race in the way the Germans went about it in the Second World war.

The deliberate and intention process of the Holocaust must go down as the single greatest evil act ever commit by man throughout time.

There can be no other parallel.

For many even to this day, it is unbelievable that an economy would be created just for the eradication of a culture and religion much older than most present-day races and religions.

It is exceedingly difficult for the German race to rejoin the normalcy of the present day when so much of their own history is caught up in the Holocaust and World War Two.

Hitler was the head of a belief not just a country and his belief was not socialism but Fascism.

He wanted the same level of existence for his own people at the expense of everybody else's people and all the countries around him.

It is no doubt that the Nazi party belonged to this same group of people hell bent on causing destruction to others around them.

They believed that they were the superior race, or the manufactured Aryan race was pure fabrication, and the tell-tale traits of Arianism, blond hair and blue eyes is more present and kin to the Nordic and Scandinavian countries than Germany.

The Germans saw something they liked and tried to replicate in their own country with little or no success.

The fact is that Hitler did not have these traits and most other Nazi party members did not have these traits.

Their belief was that the Germans were the direct offspring of Adam and eve and therefore they both must have had blond hair and blue eyes.

The Germans took it upon themselves to rid the world of anybody who was not a direct descendant of this line, and not the blood line of Jesus, or his disciples.

Germany was where after all the reformation started and therefore would be difficult to believe that the Nazi party members were atheist or agnostic were many resources were spent of safeguarding their churches and cathedrals from bombing from the allies.

If indeed they did not believe in God, then these places of worship would have been abandoned.

No doubt the Nazi party played the religious card alongside the with other methods of a superiority complex and misplaced texts and beliefs.

The German people were willing participants in the mass brain washing of their own people in the belief that the ends would justify then means.

Hitler recognised the power of religion and used it stealthily to employ his policy of the final solution on the Jewish people.

These same traits of mass culling of a population or the newly created word of ethnic cleansing was also seen in the civil war in the former republics of Yugoslavia, also seen by Saddam Hussein use of chemical weapons on the Kurds and in many African nations going through civil war.

Even though the eradication or death of prisoners which is nothing new in war has been going on for years, the unprecedented level of its use in World War Two set a new bar from which the gauntlet had been thrown down and world took many decades to recover from.

The Christian church inability to see these evil acts in history for what they really are is a difficult or growing pain that the church has been unable to move beyond.

CHAPTER 42

In the end, Jesus died an unjustified death, his punishment did not fit the crime and the concept of justice, and a civil society is based on a fair trial.

Jesus did not receive this and instead was used as an escape goat for popularism.

Although Jesus death was final, it was not the end of the story as Jesus forgave those that had betrayed him, for absolution and forgiveness to exist.

This may have been the worse outcome for all.

This approach was noticeably short, termed thinking and it is only now to we realise the limitation of this approach.

Instead of having a people who are willing to grow and learn, instead what we are left with is an endless cycle of sin and forgiveness.

We commit the same sins repeatedly only to receive absolution from are sins so that we can go on to commit the same sins again.

This seems like a fruitless existence with no justification for its continuation.

As a race their exist an inability or lack of desire to move beyond this existence and this may stem from the role that Jesus played when he was on earth.

He was a teacher as opposed to a parent.

The different may be subtle but its long-term ramifications were far greater than anyone imaged.

The reason being as any parent will testify is that as a parent there is a natural understanding that you child will grow, learn and develop with age.

The things that this same child did six months, a year or two years will not be same.

They will become more mobile, more communitive, bigger, heavier, develop all their senses to become an adult when most of their biological development will be completed.

As a parent you will have been a part of the entire process from thought to conception, to birth, to development and to guardian and so on and this is a natural part of the human development process.

As a teacher you are only getting a person for a snapshot of time from which you are trying to re-educate them or change their existing ingrained human traits or beliefs.

This is a far more difficult approach to take and Jesus sent to earth to ultimately try to set man on the right path may have found that the only way to achieve any long lasting results was to short circuit everything given the amount of time that he had to implement any change.

By short circuit, the use of miracles as a wow factor, the promise of eternal life by following his teaching, his self-sacrifice to cleanse the sins of others and the immaculate conception as a way of ensuring purity of existence in order to set out his plan for man.

In modern day we would say that he is addressing the low hanging fruit and maybe this did some good for the most part, but now the Christian church needs something more than the theatricals that Jesus brought and the promises that he made while on earth.

The forty days that Jesus spent in the dessert may have be more about seeking a new direction than dealing with present problems.

CHAPTER 43

There is no doubt that religion and religious orders have been a major factor and presence in the education of whole societies around the world whether it is Africa, Asia, the Americas, or Europe.

Christian missionaries have been there in the education and conversion of a people from paganism to Christianity and this is no more obvious than in my home country of Ireland.

In Ireland, the vast majority if not all education was conducted through religious orders.

They were responsible for the education of future leader, businesspeople, and professional people for the country for many generations.

It is only in recent times that state education or community education has become education institutions.

As a result of the huge presence of religious order in people's everyday life, the church had huge power and sway with how the country was run.

In the end of the twenty century, did the term a division between church and state become an accepted choose for most of the ruling class and population of the country.

In a Roman Catholic country, priests and bishops were responsible for your education for primary and second school levels.

It was not until you went to University or College where you are given the latitude and time to develop you own beliefs and understanding of the world around you.

Primary and second education was about learning everything off by heart and most exams were based on the ability to recall facts.

This one-way system of education where there was little room for debate or pulling apart existing theories and understanding was exactly how the church wanted everything to be.

Gods' way and will was not to be question, this is the way it is, like it or lump it.

You were not given any ability to develop within your own skin but instead given an education and qualification based on pure power of memory recall.

And this is fine if everybody else is doing it but when the Berlin wall fell and eastern Europe started opening up, many people in the west realised that the education and method of education behind the wall was not that much different to how communist schools were educating there pupil.

We were under the belief that Communism schools was about brain washing their pupil to get them to belief facts about the west history that was factually incorrect or completely out of kilter with the actual events, sand how history really occurred.

The western education systems in various countries realised that they need to move beyond data and rote learning and get people to think for themselves.

To formulate their own opinions and beliefs based on the true facts being relayed to their students.

This allowed a fuller and more well-rounded student to develop.

Not simply a student or person who was going to do exactly what they were told and not giving out or argue back to their superior or boss.

It is this exact environment and conditions that the whole area of paedophilia developed and grew.

As situations, environments or societies existed, once you were in an area of responsibility and trust you could get away with anything you liked.

You were doing god's work, and your methods and approach should not be questioned as to question your methods is to question God himself and this is something that you would not be allowed to do.

Paedophilia, ran rampant in such situations and when such issues were raised by those in authorities, the matter was pushed under the carpet and maybe could be explained away by something like, when you are doing god's work you are going to be confronted with the work of Satan and this is Satan at work, not me.

What a cope out and a load of rubbish.

Satan, a fallen angel from heaven was not about the spread of evil but was directly against how God was administering heaven and all below him.

It was a rebellion of the heavens, in which lucifer and his loyal follower fled heaven to make a new base elsewhere.

RELEGATION OF RELIGION

There are no recorded facts in any books of the Old and New Testament, that Satan was about the further destabilisation of earth and the heavens, but in fact about the preservation of the existing structure of heaven.

The fact that authorities could turn their back on the law in favour of misplaced belief is a direct result of the education system that was in place at the time.

No though was given to fact checking by the authorities if this was correct in Cannon law or belief.

The world of a priest or religious order was all that they needed.

And so, paedophilia just kept going on and on for years and decades, normally the same people committing the same offenses in different parishes, county and countries throughout the Catholic church without any method or thought to stopping or addressing these heinous crimes against the innocent.

It was not until the education system was reformed in the country did, we see priest and members of religious orders being investigated, trialled, and sentenced for their crimes.

The type of education system in the world was solely responsible for how the citizens acted and treated one another.

It was not simply good enough to say that you were doing god's work, instead the laws of the state were who you were answerable to, not your local parish priest, bishop or even Cardinal.

It may have been seen that the Catholic church just went too far and as a resulted spent the recent decade diluting their power within the state, their property portfolio and their presence within media circles and influence within the printed press.

Today, the power that the church must enact laws and influence politician has diminished and many politicians choose to distance themselves from religious order and the church as they see it not adding any benefit to their popularity.

However, this great retrenchment and change or move away has not gone unnoticed and instead or getting loyal people of religious belief doing god's work, you are now finding greater instances of corruption or mishandling of the assets of the state by politicians and civil servants.

A person without a belief is like a ship without a compass.

Every person on the planet needs a moral compass and normally this is provided by the religion that you follow.

A belief in a higher power than yourself is a way of keeping everybody in check and not running off on a tangent or a belief in a false god, cult leader, popular politician or anybody else who tries to populate the space in your brain left open and available for god and not a god figure in your life.

It is this vacuum were corruption and arrogance and all the other deadly sins inhabit in your life.

By not filling this natural void with something good, instead we are leaving is open for something bad to inhabit.

And this is exactly what happens.

Now we have politician, were before who were answerable to their Bishop, are making decision that will only help a select few or worse influenced by a lobby group that are only represent the interest of their paid clients and nobody else.

While the church represents the whole of society, politicians are only representing groups who will increase their popularity, their bank balance, or their CV.

This is a direct contrast to how the state was run when the church had all the power and influence.

This situation and scenario are replicated throughout the Christian world were the dilution of the role of the church in the running of the state has led to more instances or corruption, mishandling of state assets and war or regional conflicts.

Politicians are short term by their job's role, with most parliaments having a cap of five years.

The Catholic church may change its priorities based on the succession of a new Pope, but the Catholic church is one of the oldest institutes in the world.

In some ways has gone pass corruption and misplaced leaders, as it is aware of its role within the world and how experience trumps over the need to be popular, with doing the right thing central to the way the church conducts its business.

By its very existence, the Catholic church views all its decision in the long term or making decision based on how the world should be governed not about the way the world is governed.

It is setting an example or creating a template in which all societies should follow and adhere to.

There is no doubt that the popularity of the Catholic church has waned in the twenty first century, even if Popes were seen to embrace the marginalise or disenfranchised of society.

These groups have fallen under the banner of the Catholic church and have added their colour and texts to its overall makeup but just like a new toy if results cannot be measure or seen straight away, then this instant support starts to wane and disappear.

And an Institute that is over two thousand years old, it is exceedingly difficult to see these changes at once or even in a few years.

The most important aspect for any church in continuous loyal, true, and honest followers.

It is very easy for a person to be a follower or believer of Christ for a few years, or even a part of their life or even in around the time that they get married, but for life long followers of Christ, their rewards and more obvious and consistent.

These people are not questioning of the trials and tribulation of life, or the difficulties of daily life, but instead are accepting of the way god works, and they are able to get on with their life as such.

Major obstacles and challenges are just that, they are there to be overcome and managed head on not simply passed off or ignored as most non-believers do.

It is fairly accepting that God would want us to be challenged in everyday life so that we can understand exactly who we are and what we can do as an individual and as a group of ordinary people.

To simply not allows us to assess all our abilities or paint with all our colours is a waste or what we are and simply a child not given the chance to grow.

Every day is a new chance to grow and develop the kind of person that we want to be.

CHAPTER 44

We could see the complete opposite taking place in the time of the Khmer rouge in Cambodia were the elite and educated were systematically eradicated by a ruthless leader as a way of rolling back the progress made by it society to a time more a kin to the stone age.

The Khmer rouge did not want a class of hierarchical society but a flat managed society with a leader on top and everybody on the same level.

Although the reason for this genocide was political and not religious, with the victims being citizens of the same society, the result led to the deaths of millions and it took generations before the education level and of the whole country to be restored to a level that would be expected for a country the size of Cambodia.

Education has always been the way out of poverty and religious orders realised that in order to improve people's lives and surrounding they must be educated and brought up in a balanced way, but at the same time a controlled balanced way were they knew a little but not a lot.

In this way they would be obedient servants of Christ and the church.

The church has perfected mass control, and this sort of control has lasted for centuries.

The threat of eternal damnation and scare stories of hell was enough for most people to fall into line and do what they were told to do.

The reality is most people are just not evil enough or bad enough to get into a hell.

Hell is saved for only people that are completely born of evil.

They know no other form of existence only to be a continuous thorn in the side of the general population by frustrating people, committing deadly sins continuously without remorse, or just pure evil.

The reality for most societies is hell is going to prison.

That is there way of life and what they want to do is disrupted and they cannot live they life they want to live.

They are being punished for the crime they committed, but this decision is not gods' decision but instead the decision of judges, juries, and the courts.

They are deciding whether someone is guilt, but not if someone is evil.

Normally this opinion piece is left to the media to decide on and to generate debate amongst the population if someone's action is bad enough to warrant them to be evil.

The reality and process are simple.

Someone commits a crime, and they are arrested, trialled and if found guilty they are sentences.

However, for a person who is pure evil, they may never be found out or even trialled for a crime.

Their evil is of a different making, where they can influence other people into a life of evil acts and deeds.

Some people may say yes, this person is the devil and this is how they operate by influencing others to carry out his work but as we have already discussed, the work of the fallen angel Lucifer was not about the spread of evil but continuing on the work that he was a part of from the beginning.

His falling out with God did not suddenly propel him into going from a state of good to the direct opposite to a state of evil.

The Bible talks about evil deeds and the devil but does not attribute all evil acts to that of the devil.

There is or are obviously other actors and participants who are pushing the evil agenda at the expense of living in a world that is good and wholesome.

There can be no argument against this fact.

We have seen many evil acts committed throughout history, and it is unlikely that the whole evil agenda was created and continue by just one fallen angel and a few of his followers.

This seems a bit outlandish and unbelievable.

The reason such an alternative group of people may push the evil agenda for the basic reason of control.

They may want to develop the world in their own view, and they see the current setup and architecture as debilitating or outdated.

They may want a world with a small and more docile and obedient population.

RELEGATION OF RELIGION

The world today is complex and diverse and it is more and more difficult to get a general consensus on anything between countries even on topics which obviously need our attention, such as global warming, mass migration or destabilisation of whole regions of the world such as the Middle East or South America.

Religion at one time was a great unifying factor, especial Christianity which dominate the world affairs for generation, whether it was Catholic France, Protestants England, Catholic Spain, or Protestant Germany.

Even though these countries fought bitter wars and had major falling outs, underneath they were still followers of Christ and his work and it is no doubt that it was Christian beliefs that led to the signing of the Armistice in 1918 which led to the end of World War one, The Great War, or the war to end all wars.

When a stale mate was reached and lines were not being broken, and advances by both sides quelled, the only thing left for each side was to amend their difference and find their similarities.

And their similarities were faith and Christianity.

We only must recant the story of the brief cease fire on Christmas eve on the front line of the war when both sides lay down their arms for a moment to exchange present and well wishes with each other only for minutes later to resume hostilities.

This shows themselves and everybody else around, that something else was at play and that gods will was for the ending or this wasteful war.

Gods work was to be done and when in a brief time later an armistice was reached, there was no surprise at all amongst people as the general direction of the war supported an end to hostilities.

However, in other wars in history the outcome or reason for war has not been so obvious or easy to remedy.

The second war was no doubt a fight against good and evil, but this was not realised until allied troops found the concentration camps and figured out what was really going on.

People were not being re-educated as the Nazi propaganda said but were simply being exterminated based on their faith.

The German people, willing and continuous participants of the holocaust, must have in some way though they were doing god's work with their god being Adolf Hitler.

He had thrown a spell over the whole German people to carry out his final solution and unfortunately there is very few examples of German people going against the will of their Fuhrer and helping the Jewish people.

Instead, it was left to neighbouring countries to help the Jewish people.

Everybody of German extraction was on Hitlers side.

History ruled that Hitler must have been pure evil to plan, devise and execute such a plan.

The jokes and cartoons of his presence in hell must be of little consolation to the millions of people executed in the concentration camps and death camps.

CHAPTER 45

When Spain conquered the America's, its main aim was not just to plunder the wealth of a whole continent, but also to convert the population from their pagan religion to that of Christianity.

However, what occur was a genocide of a different sort which led to the deaths of millions of native Americas, more than was killed in the gas chambers of the second world war.

The Spanish brought disease that killed natives, executed in the thousand, people that were given the choose to convert to Christianity or be executed.

The Spanish no doubt says to themselves that they were spreading the word of God and doing god's work, so little thought was given to the consequences of their actions.

They completely changed the culture and identity of the people that they conquered in the Americas, whether it was the Inca's, Mayan or native American Indians, nobody was spared the wrath of the Spanish conquistadors and their rulers.

The King or Queen of Spain at the time was immensely powerful and was subjugated to the will of God and therefore to appease God, must continue their work unabated.

The ethnic cleaning in the name of religion went on for hundreds of years and was not just confined to a few years or decades.

The Spanish exuded their will over the Americas and saw themselves as more evolved than those of the natives, which is more superior in every way, even though most of these races and cultures were older than the country of Spain itself.

It seems that in this world to be able to stand up for oneself you need your own country and border, as has been seen with the Jewish people, Kurds in Iraq or Hutu and Tutsi in Rwanda.

Its seem that it is becoming more difficult for a distinct race to naturalise itself in a different country, which is to be part of a country identity but not necessarily part of the country's race or religion.

Each country seems to need to be pure in the eyes of some people.

That is to have cities and countries such as America, as a huge melting pots or crossroad for diverse cultures and race suited for America, but is not suited in the rest of the world.

One country, one race may soon be the calling card of a political party or movement.

To have a country with manned borders, strict immigration control to keep the exclusivity of one race, only months or years away.

There are no doubt early signs of this with Israels mass cleaning of the Gaza strip and relocation of Palestinians to sympathetic countries, in the pipeline for that region of the world.

Although there are Muslim Israeli who do identify as being Muslim but also being Israeli, this is not a trend likely to continue especially considering how the state of Israel is treating their own Muslim citizens.

They may not agree with the actions of Hamas, but to completely turn your back on your fellow Muslim is not akin to the teachings of the Koran which implores peace and gentility between each person of the Muslim faith.

On other countries such as Türkiye there is a distinct made between Kurds and followers of the PKK and citizens of Türkiye even though both groups at one stage would have be part of the same Ottoman empire.

Even people of the same faith and religion cannot always agree to live together in a peaceful and beneficial manner.

CHAPTER 46

We see this continuous theme throughout history that religion and its teaching can be more divisive that unifying.

This can be no more obvious example than in my home country of Ireland of the existence of so-called mother and baby homes where unwed pregnant women were forced to give up their newborn child to be adopted by a foreign couple unable to have children.

These couples normally came from America or the UK.

These homes which were run by various orders of nuns only came to the public's attention in the recent decades but their existence at the behest of the state went back at least to the thirties and further back in an unofficial capacity.

The state saw unwed women with a child as a problem as to have a child and be unmarried meant that you were unlikely to have a job, be able to get married or to have any semblance of a normal quality of life.

It was normally young women and teenagers who may have got pregnant, and as a result their families shunned them.

They had no other choice available to them other than to visit a convent that doubled as a mother and baby home or the proper name of Magdalene laundry.

Women were forced to work in the laundry of the convent before and after they had their baby to pay back the expense of their stay.

Some of them ended up spending their whole life in the Magdalene laundry, as just like a prison they became institutionalised at an early age and they may not have had any family or their family completely turned their back on them never to see their sister again.

The Magdalene Laundries was a government policy as opposed to any religious doctrine being force upon a society.

It is about keeping the class structure of society that was a throwback to colonial times when Ireland was part of the British empire.

Even though Ireland was and is predominately a Catholic country in the early years of the foundation of the state, the power and administration and policies of the state lay with the ruling classes and many of these Anglo-Irish business centric family had huge power over the running of the state.

As the saying goes that post boxes may have changed colour from red to green, but it was not for many decades that Irish people started to ruling Ireland as they old guard more of less died off.

The Magdalene laundry crossed the boundary between Catholic and Protestant and it was a unifying problem of Christianity.

Even though the Virgin Mary was a pregnant unwed incredibly young women, the establishment of Ireland did not want this problem replicating itself two thousand years later.

The lack of any sort of birth control and the existence in Irish culture of large Irish families meant that Irish fertility was not a problem, but in the cases were women became pregnant something needed to be done about and the Catholic church under the request of government created these mother and baby homes.

The last Magdalene laundry only closed in the late 1990's and was in the centre of Dublin city.

Everyone knew what these covenants looked like, but nobody knew the extent of what was going on behind its walls.

So, this is where the religion can be used against its own people for a harmful outcome.

Other stories becoming known about Magdalene homes is the existence of the Tuam baby plot where unborn foetus were buried in an unmarked plot in Tuam, Galway only to be rediscovered decades later.

These mass angels grave, holds the unknown number of babies who died during birth in a Magdalene laundry.

No records were kept of exactly who's baby was buried in this mass grave.

It seems unimaginable that now such a situation would exist.

Yet this is exactly what we have, a mass grave of unborn babies in the west of Ireland, that in the last number of weeks has just been exhumed.

Many of the dead babies go back to as far as the 1960's and further.

It was easier to turn a blind eye to many of the country's problems then to deal with the problems head on as they arrived.

Leave these problems for another generation to sort out is misplaced and very unchristian.

The least that these baby's deserved was a proper Christian burial if having a Christian mother was their only sin.

Today, Politician's and Civil servant do not seem to have the political desire or energy to deal with the legacy of Magdalene laundry, yet the same political parties of Fine Fail and Fine Gael are in existence since the foundation of the state.

It was the previous members or parliamentary members of these pollical parties that created the Magdalene laundries.

The government merely outsourced the problem of unwed pregnant women to the Catholic church and its leaders.

This one action has contributed to Ireland becoming a Socialist state, where tens of billions is spent every year on social services.

The alternative a capitalised state, may have been a sort of tough love, but if women knew there was no safety net to becoming pregnant then there might have been less chance of them becoming pregnant in the first place.

Surrogacy was not in existence in the state at the time and even as I draft this book, legislation around surrogacy is still to make its way through the houses of parliament.

If surrogacy did exist during the period when Magdalene laundries were in existence, then a women who became pregnant could give up their baby in a more civilise manner where she would receive some financial reimbursement which she could use for education or bettering her way of life and standard of living.

In this case the Catholic church was the intermediary in the mass adoption of Irish citizens to foreign parents.

At the time anyone born in the state was an Irish citizen.

This law has since changed but even still all these babies that were put up for adoption to foreign nationalities were Irish citizens first.

They should have had all the protection of the state, but just like the young people of Ireland emigrating to the UK and America to find work and a better life, now this was starting at and even earlier age, when they were just out of their mother's womb.

Looking back at this as an Irish citizen, this is disturbing and worrying that something like this could happen.

When the iron curtain fell and people saw what Ceausescu of Romanian was doing to his own citizens, thousands of babies locked up in orphanages, spending twenty-four hours a day lying in a cot with little or no human contact.

The people of Europe were sad, shocked, and upset that a country would treat its own citizens like this.

Yet in Ireland this was happening for decades.

We were exporting our problems to another country. Our problem, just like the British had found in the 1840's before the potato famine, that Ireland had too large a population for the limited resources it had to feed its people.

The potato famine led to the population of the country, dropping by about three million citizens, either by death or migration.

Having children was or should only be confined to the rich or wealthy class who could afford to have them in the first place.

The shape of the modern Irish family has changed drastically in the last hundred years, with people choosing not to have large families.

Most families will consist of two or three children, and this is a direct result of the cost of living not religious factors.

Not being able to give your child the best that is available is a play on most Irish parents' minds, and to give them the best, you just going to have to have less children.

Although the traditional family unit of mother, father and children is the most common family unit, economics and politics has trumped over religious belief and teachings.

RELEGATION OF RELIGION

The legacy of the Magdalene laundry is that we are still only dealing with the problems of their existence in the first place, and many of the main actor and decision makers of this era are long since dead.

The delay of introducing birth control in conjunction with women being sent by their parish priest to a Magdalene laundry to give birth to their child, so that the neighbour would not know.

Many times when a female family member, who had become pregnant, disappears for a period of time, and then reappears, an elaborate story is created, to cover up the fact that she became pregnant and had her baby in a Magdalene laundry.

Such stories would be that she was visiting a family member abroad, such as America, was in the big city work in a job, or was caring for a sick relative.

All these lies were spun merely to save face and not to have the neighbours gossiping, when in most cases a nod and wink meant that young Mary became pregnant and 'you know what happened'.

This narrow mindedness and short sightedness are a legacy of the history of Ireland and is how people acted.

It was better to spin an elaborate lie to the people you see every day, then to tell the truth in the first place.

Now in Catholic Ireland, how was this action so Christian.

It created double standards in religion which echoed through the whole Christian religion of lies, cover ups and corruption.

If you are going to start lying about becoming pregnant and having a baby, then you are going to lie about bigger things as you progress through your life.

The Priest may have even been telling lies on your behalf to smooth the transition of pregnancy.

This is what exactly happened.

Society accepted lies as just part of life and now it was accepted that Politicians could tell lies to the people that it stood for and get away with it.

It was just accepted as part of life.

This inability to tell the truth no matter what problem is staring at you is a human fallacy and sin.

It goes against all Christian values, and the problem is not about the problem itself but instead, that something that is fundamentally missing from the human psyche.

We are shown to be a week character of mind, body and spirit and our continuous need to kick for touch when what seems an unsurmountable problem arrives at our door, shows us that we have a long road ahead to becoming the vision that god see us at.

We have been weakened, down but not out, yet scared by the scandal that is the Magdalene laundry affair.

CHAPTER 47

The scandals that have plagued the Catholic Church seemed to have shaken the church but has not brought it down as many others may have thought or hoped for.

There is no doubt that the Catholic church has enemies, being a sovereign state, wealthy, with a large following and owning large property portfolio, it is going to draw the attention from other countries and organisation who would love nothing more than to see the demise of either a competitor, a long standing adversary or just simply just a jealous person.

It is to this environment that the scandals within the catholic church are born, ripped, and are brought to fruition.

It could be said that external actors to the church are encouraging this kind of activity by bringing attention to way ward followers of Christ.

No more obvious example is the case in my own home country, of Bishop Eamon Casey, Archbishop of Tuam who fathered a son with his housekeeper and siphoned of church funds to pay for his up-bringing.

When the media broke the story, the whole story became a media circus and the women at the attention of the scandal, Annie Murphy, went on national television, gave interviews, and milked the story for all its worth.

Although the two male actors of the story, the father and son, kept out of the media and refused to give any interviews, which is still the case to this day, the damage had been done.

The debate in the national media was not about celibacy, but how a figure of authority and trust within the Catholic church could turn his back on all that is holy and Christian and break his vows and commit sin, all in the name of love.

Whether it was love of lust we may never know, as the Bishop in question never publicly commented on the affair and has since passed on, but this scandal opened the door for the media to start digging into the affairs of the Catholic church in Ireland.

This brought to the attention of paedophilia within the catholic church and the continuous drip drip by the media of one story of abuse after another within the church.

The media had a field day at the expense of the Catholic church and since then all these scandals came out, church attendance is down, many churches are closing or amalgamating with other church.

The number of priests being brought into the church every year is down to single figures, and all this can be attributed to the scandals within the church.

This is in a country, often referred to as Catholic Ireland, were the church had massive power and sway over people's lives.

The fact that these cases of abuse within the church were covered up and buried, with many victims not receiving treatment at the time when it would have been most beneficial in their lives, is another scandal.

No acknowledgement was given by the press of the decent work that the church has done since Saint Patrick brought Christianity to Ireland from Whales centuries ago.

The church was responsible for educating generations of Irish people, myself included, both in primary and secondary education, encouraging trade and travel between countries, educating people and the administration of government, as when the British left in the 1920's the only people who had any administration experience in the country, was the church, through the building of churches and schools creating long term jobs.

For a small country, the list was endless yet when the scandal of abuse broke, all this was forgotten about and the gossip wheel took over, and any man wearing vestiture's was a target.

Now you looked at your parish priest with a shifty eye, thinking is he one of them, all within the space of a few years.

It went from the fear of God in you if you were every rude to your priest, to now having your own personal agenda that said any man of the cloth was to be treated the same.

This has led to a dilution of goodness and a moralistic person within our country.

Everyone was in the same boat, if you committed one sin or a hundred sins, it did not matter.

We were all being tarred with the same brush and this can only be attributed to the work of the media, both the printed press which really went about and hounded member of the catholic church, to the television channels which ran endless documentaries and interviews about this scandal and that scandal.

RELEGATION OF RELIGION

The fact is the church is a mirror of the society that it inhabits. The teachings of Christ are just that, with the most important one, forgiveness never given a chance in public.

Christs arrival on earth was god's way of forgiving his own people for their sins.

The cities of Sodom and Gomorrah were creations by man not god, original sin in the garden of Eden was again, womenkind's sinning, Kaine killing his brother Abel was also one of the greatest sins of them all, so god is acknowledging that man does and will sin and that forgiveness is a part of this cycle.

However with scandals within the church, it seems that the church had fallen within the eyes of the common man and women and they were exacting their revenge on the church for instances of corporal punishment, which was legal in the country up until the end of the last century.

It was like the media had the church in a vice and they were holding on for dear life as they were not going to get a better story than this.

The church came out of the affair, battered, and bruised, a little poorer with a little less land, but the church had learnt the most important lesson of them all, the church knew who its friends were and who its enemy were.

It was not simply about now a battle against good and evil, the work of the devil or a demon, it was institutions set up by man who had a clear agenda to destabilise and bring down the church.

This was noticeably clear.

Wayward and sinful priest was more plentiful than ever before.

Within the space of a few years' paedophilia ran rampant with in church in Ireland, America, Canada and Australia and the root of this spell of paedophilia still has not been found.

For centuries you had priests, follower of Christ with no cases of paedophilia being reported, to suddenly within a few decades of one century of the churches twenty centuries of existence, paedophilia coming to the fore and being covered up.

The cover up stems from the fact that there was no prior history of something like this happening within the church and therefore, it can only be caused by an external force, actors, or organisations.

The brotherhood of the priesthood stems from Jesus last meal, or last supper on earth.

With this he broke bread and drank wine as a symbol of his complete sacrifice for his people.

Only by giving himself entirely, could he save his people from whatever wrath god had planned, just like what was exacted against the cities of Sodom and Gomorrah, or in the times of the great flood and Noah, or against the pharaoh in Egypt.

Gods will be done and if not done then there are consequences.

Jesus arrival on earth was quite possible a last chance salon for the people of Palestine and when they did not take to Jesus all Jesus was left with was the ultimate sacrifice, his own body for the people he loved.

It is from this backdrop that the brotherhood of priest, or the catholic church stems from.

The are what stands between God and the wiping out of humankind.

Humankind continues to sin again with little hope of a change in course.

The only hope for man is to follow Jesus' teachings.

And it is through the Eucharist and the Holy Communion that we replicate the last supper and the ultimate sacrifice that Jesus made for us.

So, when we look at the Catholic church and formulate our opinion, we need to look at the whole history of the church not just analyse a snapshoot in time of events in a few countries and a few decades.

There is no possibility of trying to water down the events that occurred on the Catholic church watch, when educating the children with which they were entrusted.

Paedophilia and the abuse of children is the worst sin of them all.

Children's growth becomes stunted, they are unable to escape the cycle of events in their head, and their own lives are affected.

The perpetrators of the events must be found, tried, and punished, and valuable lessons must be learnt as to how these events occurred in the first place.

These lessons must have fixed, and implementable solutions were something like this is never allowed to happen again.

However, in the same breath we should not allow our way of life, the teachings of Christ and the institution that is the Catholic church fall because of a few bad apples.

RELEGATION OF RELIGION

When we look at the event of paedophilia in Ireland and the U.S., we can see that it is the same names and people that keep cropping up and that are reported on repeatedly.

It was the hope that by moving these priests onto a different parish, that they would also be moving out what ever evilness was in the priest that was causing them to commit these sins in the first place.

This is the greatest failing of the church, to have this as a thought, action, and policy.

If anybody in any workplace is under investigation for any wrongdoing, their work is normally suspended, and they are not allowed to go around doing their normal duties.

They are reassigned to something that is less forward facing until the investigation is concluded.

This is normal practise.

To move a priest during an investigation for such a serious offense, is against all moral and legal best practises.

This was the single greatest failing of them all as a level playing field could not be set up for a safe and impartial investigation to continue.

As a result, normal charges were dropped, or the victims recanted the allegations against the priest in question.

This further delayed the course of justice, and it would now be many decades before the true extent of the crimes against children by priests of the catholic church would become known.

This kicked the can down the road for another generation to deal with the problems and bottled up everything until it came out front news on all the major newspapers around the world.

The major broadsheets and tabloids took the story as far as it goes, always saying that it was in the public interest to see how far and how wide these abuses went and how far up the chain of command within the Catholic church did the abusers go up and how far did the knowledge of the abuse go.

When the dust settled on the breaking of the story, it was clear that the Pope, the College of Cardinal's, and most of the holy see knew that this abuse was occurring.

The problem was as these abuses were caught early enough, known about or certainly suspicious raised, the abuser where always front-line workers where they had the greatest exposure to child.

As within any organisation the higher you go up the less front line of a worker you are, spending more time on administration and management, which is what the job of the Pope is all about.

The lower down you are, the more of your time is spent on front line and day to day issues.

In any organisations or situations, this is perfectly normal, however when the crime and sin is about exposure to children and having the time and space to have your way with, a priest, of any role within the church has the greatest exposure.

A bishop is spending more time on administration, and this is the case the further you go up.

Being a priest and a paedophile, is a perfect cover and grounds to commit your crime.

As for cover, the existence or repentance and sin, means that you can repeat the same offenses repeatedly and get away with as long as possible.

Even if the legal and criminal agencies are brought in, as the Vatican is a sovereign state with its own legal system, this can be used as a cover or excuse to internally dealing with perpetrators without the public knowing anything was going on in the first place.

The Catholic church is good at keeping secrets and there has always been a veil of secrecy around and over the Catholic church which has given rise to many conspiracy theories over the years.

It is within this eco system and environment, that once a priest joins and starts to display paedophilia tendencies, it is very difficult to correct the situation or bring an end to the situation as would happen to a person in any other profession or jurisdiction.

The church spends more time protecting its own than the people that they were entrusted to protect in the first place.

It is this backdrop that many people have loss faith and belief in the church.

CHAPTER 48

However, this faith and belief is confined to the walls and buildings and administration of the Catholic church, and now to the teachings and lessons within the bible, which through all the times that abuse was reported, sales of the bible and other religious material did not drop, in fact it actually increased.

People took it upon themselves to be their own preacher.

They came to the belief they did not need an intermediary or reinterpreted to explain what was written down for them in every spoken language and text that had been around for thousands of years.

More people took it upon themselves to read the bible, not just piece together the various stories and lessons of the bible from weekly readings and other religious ceremonies.

They needed to know for themselves first-hand what the need for Jesus in their lives.

What happen was a sort of second reformation period for the Christian church that is going on now and has been going on for the last decade.

People are shopping around the major and off shoot religions as well as religions based on different interpretations of the bible, however most people will not stray too far from where their religious beliefs were from an early age.

They will mostly stay within the Christian world of religion albeit with a different spin, context, or reinterpretation.

People who convert to Islam or Buddhism, first need to find a sort of commonality that exists between their former religion and the religion to which they are converting.

That is, they need to feel that they are not just jumping into something with both feet because it is new or feels good and fresh but that there are a meaning and space for the religion within their lives.

That by converting they know they will be joining a new community and new way of life and may very well be leaving behind friends and family to convert.

For some people who are unattached this may be easy, but for other people who feel abandoned by their religion and faith, where all meaning has lost resonation within their lives.

They feel that they need to do something, as there is a void that is growing inside them, and they need to fill it within something before their lives become hollow and empty.

Religion can take up as much and as little of you time that you give it and what people find, it is when they make space for religion in their lives, it makes space for them and they increasingly see the need for a constant religious presence in their lives.

The void becomes less pronounced and noticeable once they manage their spiritual requirements.

To try to use other mechanisms to distract the human soul for the desire to feed your religious well-being is just a distraction mechanism and becomes fruitless and wasteful as time progresses.

Some people are unaware of this void existing in the first place and may confuse it with something else, such as the need to have a romantic partner, the need to travel, a mini mid-life crisis where you start to question your life up until this point, not feeling you have done anything good with your life or just the inability to independently self-assess your life and see the things that you need to work on.

We simply cannot be a race or species that meanders through life, going day to day without critical assessment or formulating a plan to where we are going with our lives.

The hippy movement spawned from people giving up on the existing trappings of life, such as job, career, marriage, government, parents, and mainstream society, to carve out something new for them that was based on the universal acceptance that God loves us.

The hippy period and generation which is still in existence and which ended up contributing plenty to mainstream culture, were people realising that there had to be more to life than just living nine to five, paying bills, raising children and living a fairly hum drum existence.

They wanted to break the Mold, and although many of the practise went against most of the major religions beliefs and teaching, the spirit of what the hippy movement was trying to put across or relay was very much in keeping with Christian values and the values of all the other main stream religions.

The hippy culture was very much instrumental in creating start up culture and entrepreneurialism as well as many of the founders of tech companies in silicon valley got their inspiration or desire to go on their own as opposed to taking a job with a big corporations from the hippy culture and this culture is still found throughout California based companies even to this day.

Religion is not just about following a specific set of beliefs, teaching, stories, and lessons but practising what is being taught by the Bible, Torah or Koran as the way to live your life.

RELEGATION OF RELIGION

Not every single lesson has to be taken at face value but just applied to your own life in a remarkably simple and transparent way that makes you see the benefit that religion in your life can bring.

Religion is not the justice system of a country, the moral high ground of a country or to voice of reason or go to place for a person.

Religion is a self-service help centre, were when a person is running low or feels that the world, society and man is just simply against them and nothing is going right for them, simply picking up a book may recentre you negativity and bring a more positive outlook for your life during a difficult period.

Religious faith does not require maintenance but there will be times when you need it more than others and these times is when you are losing confidence in yourself and those around you.

This loss of confidence may get you addicted to some drug as an outlet, but this is only a temporary solution to a deeper problem.

For people who have gone considerable time or portions of their lives without recentring their religious belief, they have a longer and higher road to climb, and they will need to dig deeper again to right what is wrong in their lives.

For person who are lapsed in whatever religion they were originally part of, they may feel the time is too long to return to their faith and religion.

Little do they realise that it is this exact people, where religion will benefit them.

They will need to throw out what is old or not working in their lives when they return to their church or pick up their religious book and return to a place of worship and attend a religious ceremony such as a wedding or funeral.

The faith that is required by us in order to follow and be followers of a religion requires some self-sacrifice on our part, that is we must give up something to get something in return and what we get in return will be more beneficial and worthwhile and needed then what we were willing to give up in the first place.

You give a little, you get a little and this is the story of religion.

It is not one big bang, or one quick solution, but the simple building up on an individual's faith based on the teachings and lessons of a prophet or religious leader.

The world is currently running low on morals and ethics and good practises.

People have lost their way and just like the good shepherd leading his sheep to greener pastures, it is needed for each individual persons to analyse their lives and enact active and positive changes.

People think that volunteering for a good cause or giving money to charity is some sort of religions mainstay or tenant and although the act of goodness and kindness is important in all religions, the most important part or act, is acknowledging that you are not alone in the world and that you as an individual are the only person that can make real and lasting changes to your life and to the lives of those around you.

The void that people experience in times in their lives is just part of growing up and maturing as an adult.

Unfortunately, many people who are victims of abuse are unable to experience this natural progression of life and are frozen in a time in the past that they are unable to move past.

This is the legacy of abuse in countries such as Ireland and the U.S. where people's childhoods have been stolen by paedophiles masquerading as disciples of God and doing his work.

They manipulate the words of the Gospel and the Bible to suit their own agenda and even are so brazen to argue that paedophilia is accepted practise in the bible as young teenagers were able to marry and have children.

How ever the laws of each country say differently, and it is to the laws of each country that Priest and Preachers of the various faiths are bound by.

This stolen childhood has far reached and far lasting ramifications for the individuals in questions and the subsequent relationships that people have.

Many victims of abuse have had marriage breakdowns, divorces and separations and joint custody of their children.

The damage done at an early age cannot be undone and the only course of treatment is acceptance of the events in their full without understanding why they happened in the first place.

In many countries were abuse by the church has occurred, the church has been responsible or required by law or agreements with respective governments to fund and pay for therapy and counselling for victims of abuse as well as paying some sort of compensations.

This has required the church sell lands and building that they are not using and merging their property holdings.

RELEGATION OF RELIGION

This money generated from the sale of land that the church may have had for many years, is funded to various programme and initiatives for the victims of abuse.

This has required the church taking a backward step and giving up control of the running of schools and hospitals that they may have owned and ran, and which was a part of the church's annual income.

The Catholic church in many countries is a pale comparison of its former glory and does not have any of the same power or sway in countries where it was entrenched for many years.

Legislation that was not allowed to be passed due to the Church's presence and position, such as abortion, divorce and marriage equality are now being quickly pass and adopted in the European countries in the last decade which is in keeping and in tandem with the dilution of power of religion within these same countries.

The position of the church has now been ignored by politician, and once where they would go to their Bishop to seek his position on such a political matter is long gone.

The church can now only give an opinion as to what its followers should do in such various matters and not rule from above but from the side lines.

This advises is completely lost in the noise of modern-day life, but its position of unquestioned authority has been completely removed as a factor that most countries where Catholicism it the majority religion is.

Is there is a road back to its former glory or does the church want to regain the moral high ground that it occupied before.

The Church sees that the message that Jesus was sent to relay to us has been around for two thousand years and more and that although this message is the absolute unpinning and foundation of the Catholic church and Christianity in general, it must have relevance and resounded in each and every person that its words fall on.

There is no point in a priest regurgitating texts from the Bible week in and week out only to have little or no effect.

The Catholic church is expecting people to fall out with the church at some point, to become a lapsed catholic but in later life when the need arises to rediscover and reaffirm their belief in the church and in the teachings of Jesus.

This is something of a modern take on Jesus' teachings, but it is a realistic and honest assessment of where the church is at these days.

For the Church itself to grow in spirit and faith it needs to decide its relevancy and place within the modern-day world.

It has gone from being the largest single service provider of education and healthcare in the world to an organisation that has a number of different service providers.

The church still owns a huge private property portfolio in the world and still lends its name to many educational institutions, but it is no longer the same presence in education than before, with many state, semi-private and private organisations and entities taking over the running of schools and hospitals.

The income that the church did receive from these service providers is no longer the steady stream that it had been before.

This in result has affected the ability of the church to provide services in less profitable services such as providing for the homeless or the poor.

As a direct result of the Catholic church stepping back from the services it provides as a direct result of abuses committed by priest to its followers, many governments and agencies have had to step in to provide these same services, normally in more expensive and less cohesive and efficient manner.

The church was and still is particularly good at getting the maximum value from its money and people that provide these services.

No report is available which compares the services provided by the Catholic church and their associated cost and the service and provided by the agencies that had to step in provide these same services.

This has had the counter effect of the governments increasing their debt to GDP ratio especially during Covid times when in previous epidemics that did not occur.

The church did provide many of the same services at a fraction of the cost.

This debate has not occurred in government circles or the debate why such a service is costing a lot more than it did before.

One of the main reasons is the church did not have problems attractive unpaid volunteers to provide these services.

RELEGATION OF RELIGION

There was no vetting of individuals before they worked in high-risk areas.

Once the Priest or Bishop thought you were all right and could do the job, then you were in.

It is this breach of trust and betrayal by persons masquerading as followers of Christ that is where some of this abuse occurred.

Lay people, that is people not directly affiliated with the religious orders started to become more prevalent or accepted within the services of the Catholic church, proving the same frontline service that a religious cleric would normally provide, such as teaching around the same time that cases of abuse were being reported.

It is strange to think that all cases of paedophilia were committed by people from a religious order and that none came from the unvetted volunteers or lay people that the church took on to provide services and administration to many services that they provided.

All statements of abuse were against people from a religious order.

If you take a cross section of the population and cases brought to the criminal courts in any country, were in recent years sexual abuse case has been on the rise.

The overwhelming number of cases are against the common person or women.

The legacy case of abuse by Priests has either being dealt with or justice has been done.

The only interpretation is that the Catholic church has done an amazing job in stamping out paedophilia within in its ranks in the space of a brief time given the length of time that the Catholic church has been in existence.

Otherwise, somebody was fudging the numbers along the way.

The fact that most sexual crimes are now committed by the average person and women and in some cases, child, there has been a complete flipped from the days when all sexual crime was being carried out by men of the cloth.

Is this another case of a cover up or the media spinning the facts.

The reality is no society changes that quickly that the sins of crime are being pass onto a different genre of society.

The fact that an unchanged organisation for thousands of years and yet within a few decades is seen to be running rampant with paedophilia can only draw suspicion and wonder as to what the real facts of the situation are.

Has the Catholic church become a pawn in a bigger game of international espionage and politics.

Did the church allowed itself to be used in such a way that caused long term and irretrievable damage to its reputation and besmirched the demanding work of the faithful and its followers.

One can only hope that this is not the case, but it is becoming more difficult to explain this occurrence when looking at all the data and by using the power of artificial intelligence.

By inputting the data in various algorithmic generated engines using data and training sets provided by victim support agencies in various countries, there are more questions than answer that need to be provided.

The Catholic church cannot become an escape goat for the actions of another organisation who may have their own agenda.

Their agenda to rule the world and exercise control over people which is becoming more and more of a problem either by big business, big government or international affiliated cartels and gangs who control the lives of millions of people directly or indirectly through narcotics, people smuggling or control of shell companies to launder dirty money.

Since the church took a backward step in the lives of billions around the world, this is left the door open for more dubious characters and organisations to step in a fill the void left by the once all-powerful Catholic church.

This has led to great regional destabilisation and the greatest mass migration since the Second World War.

One can only wonder what the world would have looked like if paedophilia was never a problem or in existence within the Catholic church.

CHAPTER 49

No book would be complete without covering the religion and politics that divide a nation and to this day partition is still a reality on the island of Ireland.

When Saint Patrick came from Wales to Ireland to convert the natives from paganism to Christianity nobody could have foreseen the consequences that lay ahead.

At the time there was no dominant religion on the island, but instead native Irish people, Celts believed in their own set of pagan gods that were primarily based around the seasons.

Irish gods stem from her relationship with mother nature and how the change in seasons being harvesting of crops to the farmers.

Such important milestones in the calendar were celebrated such as the summer and winter equinox and no greater example of this can be seen in Newgrange where the winter solstice is celebrated as the mechanism of being the shortest day of the year.

It is seen as the start of new life and new beginnings.

Other festival, such as Halloween is about celebrating the dead and it is when the dead can Passover into the land of the living.

Irish pagan religion is based on the understanding and relationship with the underworld and the land of the dead.

Much time was and still taken to caring for the dead in Ireland both in their last moments, in the morning process and in the graveyard where there are buried, decades and centuries after they have been interred.

Many old graveyards are managed and taken care of even if the last burial was hundreds of years ago.

Irish people and its culture have a close association if not twinning with death and the underworld.

It is to this environment where Saint Patrick was sent to as a missionary, where druids not priest ruled over their people and there was no uniformity to how people practised their beliefs.

Their pagan gods were numerous and diverse as the season that they brought and to try and change a islands belief from belief in many gods to the belief in one god made up of three parts, the holy Trinity, was going to be an uphill struggle.

Yet hundreds of years later, the complete opposite occurred, where Irish people became almost fanatical followers of Christianity which then became Catholicism, which is when all the issues of religion on the island came to the fore.

As we are all too aware of, Ireland was part of the British Isles and ruled by the King and Queen in London.

As Ireland sat beside a much more powerful neighbour, just like Wales and Scotland it was unable to shake of the dominance of the English and Norman influence.

Ireland was for a longer part of its history a divide nation made of small kingdoms and clans each with their own head and capital.

Land was gained through invading a neighbour and this see sawing effect went on for hundreds of years.

When the English saw Ireland as an agriculture base which would support their increasing populations and cities, then Ireland was quickly invaded and taken over by the English.

This started an occupation that lasted eight hundred years.

During this time Ireland had moved from a pagan based society to a Christian based society.

When the church in Rome would not allow King Henry the eight to divorce his Queen, then King Henry embraced the religious revolution that had begun in Germany by Martin Luther.

Protestants was the name given to protesters of the church in Rome aligned to the Pope.

Henry wanted himself as head of his own church, the church of England and so as subjects of the English King, Irish people were required also to change their religion.

Although Irish people had converted already from paganism to Christianity, this was going to be a bigger ask from which Irish people refused to change their religion to Protestant and instead maintained their allegiance to the Pope in Rome.

The King and subsequent Kings and Queens all tried to address this Irish problem.

As other dominions in their realm did not seem to have the same problem why did Irish people not want to convert to Protestants.

RELEGATION OF RELIGION

Through such initiatives as the penal laws, which banned the practising of Catholicism of any form on the island, to the various plantations of Protestant people aligned to the head of church in England, England wanted Ireland to become wholly Protestant just like mainland Britain was.

To Britain, Ireland was a thorn in their side that needed to be dealt with and when the potato famine came along in the 1840's and the London government was slow to act in helping its people, the Catholic population of Ireland shrunk from eight million to just over five million.

This is what the population is today in the south of the country.

The population once fell as low as three and a half million, the lowest under British occupation, which was the consequences of years of occupation and anti-Catholic policies by the London government.

It is from this environment, that religious tensions were born on the island when religion was never a divisive factor on the island before.

The fact that this all stems from King Henry's inability to produce a son is very much a cause of disagreement to this day between Dublin and London.

Many lives were lost or destroyed because of one mans need to dominate.

Other heads of monarchy, such as Elizabeth I, knew how divisive an heir to the throne could be and decided to deliberately opt out of the need to have an heir and let others decide the fate of the country after her death.

To this day, the monarch of England is also the head of the church, there is no division between church and state in England, Wales, Scotland, and Northern Ireland.

Although belief and faith has changed and church attendance dramatically dropped in the last century, power has not be distributed to the arch Bishop of Canterbury who would be seen as the natural head of the church of England but instead gods rule must be maintained by the monarch.

Irish politics and religion is therefore very much intertwined with that of Britain, and this brought about the troubles in Northern Ireland, were division was not based on colour and creed which we saw in America and south Africa, but on the two different strands of religion, Catholic and Protestant,

Each religions teachings was the same and both sides and they prayed to the same god, but on purely political grounds, were Unionist saw their head of the church as the head of the monarch, were Catholics saw their head of the church as the Pope.

Catholics in the north did not and do not see the south as their natural alliance, purely for the fact that the south is predominately Catholic, but instead saw and see the north as their home which they unwillingly must share with Protestants who control most of the powerful jobs, roles and administration within the province.

Catholics in the north are not per see directly aligned with Dublin, as present day discussions about a united Ireland, where both the north and south have one political body, centres not about religious divide and beliefs but the economic cost that it would cost to united the island of Ireland.

Nobody wants anyone to take a lap of honour if the day comes when a united Ireland is a reality, but instead both sides want a future that is peaceful and happy.

The south in recent years has changed, when once it was almost completely Catholic, about ninety five percent of the population at one stage, to a more multi-cultural society, where your religion or where your from is not as important compared to previous generations.

As a result, accepting of another person based on their religion is a much easier prospect.

It is this backdrop where present day discussions are at, however as politicians tote up the cost of a united Ireland, it may be a generation or two before this becomes a reality.

As the south's economy has propelled in recent decades, the northern economy is heavily dependent on government, and civil servant jobs as well as large subsidies from the British economy, the obstacle is cost not religion.

As we look at religious upheaval in Ireland over the last centuries, we wonder what it was all about.

What was gained bar for the fact that the monarchy in London became a more powerful person, the same trick used by the Romans and Emperor Constantine, when the Roman empire adopted Christianity as their chosen religion dropping their pagan gods, where many moneys had been spent on temples for the pagan gods over the previous centuries.

These temples where then converted in church many centuries after Jesus was born, born into a province of Rome in the Roman occupied Middle East.

RELEGATION OF RELIGION

When the Caesar realised that Christianity was growing so big that it could one day take over Rome, which it did by the presence of the Vatican in Rome.

Quickly the Caesar realised, that he needed to shift gears and start backing a different horse, which being Christianity.

CHAPTER 50

It is the case that religion is being used as an extension of political power throughout times, not just in the middle ages and it is from this that people started developing the god complex, like the case of Hitler or Pol Pot or other genocidal maniacs who think they are god and can do what they like.

It is not the case that they are doing god's work but are God in its entirety.

The lack of division between political, military, and religious power is sadly lacking in many countries and when you have one person controlling these powerful strands of administration, you are going to get deadly consequence.

This is because man is not the architect of his own destiny and is unable to distinguish between the different demands and responsibility required of these three modern day compressed powers.

Even the Pope possess these three powers, being the head of a sovereign state, then head of a standing army as well as the head of the Catholic church whose members numbers are in the billions.

So much power compressed into the hands of just one person, and people who get into these positions have little oversight or other people looking over their shoulders to see what their next move could be.

As the adage goes, absolute power corrupts absolutely, and this is what we see repeatedly throughout history and time.

The abuse of any form has been going and is going on for generations and the consolidation of power into an individual's hands only makes this more of a reality.

The use of the decision-making process by consensus such as democracy and socialism has done little to abate this consolidation of power into one person.

A person who is a believer in any of the three major religions is of the belief of a mono theistical God, which is one God who is the ultimate superpower over all that exists.

It is with this that with the delusion of religion or to put it into better terms, the relegation of religion, a vacuum or space has been created in people's lives.

This is where God has been replaced or superimposed by another being and that could be a politician, celebrity, sports player, or some other high profiled person that the media and advertising companies are pushing as the next important thing.

People's attention has been intentional shifted away from religious heads and more specifically God and onto, what we can call lesser beings, who overnight in people's minds are seemed to be superhuman with superhuman tendencies.

These same people are taught how to court the media and the public at large and are seem to come across and humbling and overwhelmed by their popularity and public attention that they are receiving.

All along this is what their agent's, public relation consultant and manager are aiming for.

That they become more marketable to the advertising companies so that they get the contracts to endorse the big products, such as Nike, Adidas, or other lines of business where there high public profile can be used.

Most of this artificially inflated public persona can be linked to the creation and evolution of the Paparazzi specially created around the British royal family by the likes of Rupert Murdock tabloids and broadsheets.

Rupert Murdock really wanted to shake up the British establishment and we saw the British natural tendency to gossip about others as a well to exploit society and to sell more papers.

And this is what he did.

As the role of religion was taking a dip in most people's lives, the upward trajectory of celebrity status, overnight stars and increased intrusion into people's lives was on the up.

Now, instead of people buying newspapers based on political, economic or sports news, people were now buying papers based on what member of the royal family was doing, what a specific football was now worth or what music star was doing in a hotel room.

The changing of the guards, with an obvious shift in people's morals away from Christian beliefs to morals and beliefs exposed by newspapers, the media and various television channels, has been the start of a downward spiral for most modern day western cultural countries.

People have swapped out their Christian values for something more plastic, less tangible, and more destructive.

RELEGATION OF RELIGION

Now people are bombarded daily by useless news, that is news that is irrelevant to the situation that people are living, factually inaccurate, that is fake or misleading news, or hopeful or wishful or fanciful news and programming were people can escape the reality of their lives and worlds that they are currently live and enter some sort of fake universe where they allow their minds to dream and hope.

Unfortunately, most people will never have the lives, houses, cars, and other materialistic goods that the media and television channels are pushing as obtainable to everybody.

Simply the economics do not add up to this utopian lifestyle that everybody wishes for, yet if you watch any sort of television, this is what is being peddled night, noon, and morning.

We have gone from a Christian society to a materialistic society in a noticeably short space of time, without most people realising it.

Our new god is television and has been for a number of decades.

Now even we do not know any other form of society or structures to our lives.

Our lives are just too busy, and too wasteful for us to notice or to do anything about it.

Religion that was once the anchor and fixed point in most people's lives, which gave structure and consistency and familiarity is gone and replaced by something that is flimsy, inconsistent, and unloving.

And this mass movement to consumerisation can be attributed to big business and the sales and marking of products by companies.

Employing a high-profile sports star to help sell you more runners, jerseys or electronics does not make the products any better or make it more apprehensible for a person.

It is simply making a person believe that if I buy this product then I will be more like such and such a celebrity or sports star.

This is simply not true and all you are doing is lining the pockets of the already rich advertising executives and company director who will all share in increased sales and profits.

Religion has not just taken a back seat in people's lives, but it has completely been replaced altogether by consumerisation.

You think, well this is nothing news and we have known about this for a long time, and people are recognising this form of life and existence and are making changes to their lives to have something more tangible and sustainable.

However, this change, as much as it is welcomed and warranted, sees people not returning to their roots in religion of God but being more aware of the environment and the people around them.

This takes the form as becoming more environmental conscious, by recycling, using public transport, not buying a car, cutting down of foreign holidays, all in the name of cutting down their carbon footprint.

But this action is a reaction to the fact that the planet is getting warm like the scientists warned us thirty off years ago and in order to save our own skin, we actually need to be doing something and that is reducing are carbon footprint.

The other approach is the uptake in mental or conscious aware programme such as Yoga, Pilates, and meditation.

That is where people try to tap into their mind and body in the hope that they can achieve some inner peace and harmony.

Unfortunately, as much as celebrities and other high-profile people rave on about the benefits and result of Yoga or Pilates or Mediation, these forms of therapy have been in existence for thousands of years.

They are nothing news, they are not a trend or fad but something that has been part of religion since its inception.

This is the results of the commercialisation of the various aspects of religious life.

In order to have a relationship with god you need to overcome the failings of the human body, and the only way to overcome its failing is to have control over your body and mind through strict discipline which is something that monks and nuns and priest have been practising for thousands of year.

The absence of sex and devotion to God by priests and nuns is just one example and this natural human urge and desire can be controlled through mediation, exercise, and body movement.

These approaches can also deal with stress and anxiety and just simply cleansing the mind to make way for other aspects of life that are more beneficial such as healing of the sick and poor, charity work or dealing with the dark under belly of society, the parts of society that religious orders have been dealing with for hundreds of years, but the average persons does not want to know about or just completely avoids.

Such religion as Buddhism, Yoga is directly attributed to this religion and in Japan, Pilates is a central pillar of most people's daily lives, where they start each morning stretching their bodies, knowing that a healthy body is a healthy mind.

The Japanese attribute a lot of their culture to oneness with their environment and the people around them.

They believe in a sort of collective happiness where to be happy, others around also need to be happy and if they are not you need to help them in some way.

The interlinking of their society means that they do not feel alone but part of something bigger.

And it is this that most people crave, the desire that they are in some way part of something bigger than just themselves.

To be the captain of their own ship, to have complete autonomy over all their decisions, is unfortunately not what most people want these days.

They want to be told by advertising companies and celebrities, where to eat, what to wear, where to go on holiday and what to do with their weeks.

Independent thought is no longer what it used to be, and it is like now that people are being programmed on how to live their lives.

They do not possess the autonomy of independent thought to plough their own path for their lives and this can be attributed to the fact that most people do not know what they want for their lives or what they want to get out of living.

They are stuck on auto pilot and go through each day the same as the previous week.

Anything spontaneous is already in their mind and conscious through the power of advertising.

They are not living their own lives but the life that is created through mass marking and mass media.

They are unable to break this Mold, and the absence of God and religion only makes this task and this cycle more difficult to break out of.

They are normally critical of people because they do not see what a person doing something, what happiness or joy that hobby, job, or responsibility brings that person.

They are like a building without any foundations.

On the surface it looks normal and safe but if any weather anomaly occurs or over any period, the building will start to fail and cracks will appear in the walls, the building may subside and quickly becomes unsafe.

After a while the building will be declared uninhabitable and unsafe for human occupation.

Its tenant will be forced to make some radical alterations to their lives to move back into the building they once occupied.

In the meantime, they are homeless and looking for a safe port in the storm, which is when these same people are exploited by aspects of society.

What we are witnessing is thus the transfer of intellectual property rights from religious order, which have been established for hundreds of years to main stream business interested were they are been rebadged and sold on as new concepts or sometimes proven holistic approaches to alternative medicine.

This approach is only plain highway robbery and to pretend to sell it off when it is someone else's works or worse still a well-founded organisation work as you own is what businesses these days is all about.

The internet has been great at joining the world and making ecommerce something new, but it has also opened the door for mass consolidation of concepts and ideas.

The banks and other businesses realised this and instead of marching down the path of a few conglomerates owning everything, it made business sense to segment that market wherever possible.

As a result for example, if you want to watch a match on television, the rights holder and the broadcasting company that is showing it could be a number of different broadcasters.

This is the same for coffee shops, airlines, and holiday destinations.

Choose is no doubt abundant but it does not mean we are getting a better deal.

In fact, competition is making the marketplace worse for consumers as when all relevant actors have established themselves in the marketplace, you start to see minor difference between price and service.

A status quo is thus born and managed and goes on generating profits and spending money on numerous services without any benefit to the consumer.

This just creates an artificial economy with no economic sound footing.

At any sign of trouble, the smaller players just roll into the bigger player.

What does this business practise have to do with religion, I hear you say.

The bottom line is religion is a business like any other, and even though most religious interests are charity based thrust, they still employ people and generate revenue, even if their objectives and goals is not to make a profit but to provide services.

This is where business interest differs.

Any profits made by religious trusts charities is ploughed by into delivering improved services where in traditional businesses, profits are hived off to owners and shareholders and profit margins.

Sometimes this large profits are diluted by paying over inflated prices for professional service just to maintain the old school tie network, something that should have seen its death at the end of the last century but still has a bang and a hangover from British imperialism and their sense of superiority. Move on.

Religion is big business, and we only must look at the super churches in the U.S. and their large weekly following to see how the upgrade of Christian interpretation is reborn into something different and new.

Sunday service is an entertainment show as much as a day, time, and place to worship your god.

Some of these services lasting the entire day, with young children also attending Sunday service.

Whole families and communities, congregate for these shows and traditionalist may argue that it's just a lot of hype and exuberance that lets people feel good about themselves for a few hours, where they are a part of something bigger, they can express themselves to god differently than they would in another place of worship through song and dance and where the gulf between man and god seems to lessen.

It is probably a lot of over exuberance but it is certainly better than nothing or worshipping no god and you would hope that these same people carry out the rest of the week in the same manner and approach in the way the represent themselves when attending Sunday service.

CHAPTER 51

Most of America is made of European settlers, with the rest coming from South America, existing native Americas or the Asian countries of China and Vietnam.

When the original settlers started their campaign of wiping out the native Americas, it was in the approach to completely wipe the slate clean and start again.

Many European settlers came from failing economies, countries, war, and famine and were looking to start again in a different foreign land where few if anybody knew them or their history.

This is the backdrop that all religions based in American have to contend with and their new religions of Mormonism and Scientology which are basically closed economic and religious communities where to become a member requires signing over part of your income to these organisations or giving large recurring donations to their income.

It is the transection of religion and business is where any issues can arise.

When a religion is something more than the worship of God, and it is instead maintaining a separate parallel economy and eco system separate to the existing communities and regions that they inhabit.

You then create a us versus them mentality with anybody who is not rich enough or of a different religion to these mainstream alternative profit-oriented religions.

Although these religions will say in their accounts all monies are reinvested into the upkeep of their communities, what they are really doing is siphoning off economic activity from the mainstream economy and handing contracts and accounts to its own members to provide services.

This is a state within a state, and it is any wonder how these religions get away with it.

Although the U.S. constitution does guarantee freedom of religious expression, this does not mean going out and creating a religion which is counter to the spirit that the U.S. was founded on.

Mormonism is the best example of a separate and parallel religion and organisation, a state within a state, which being Salt Lake City Utah, the home of Mormonism.

The root of Mormonism just like most roles in life is the transcendence or elevation of the soul to a higher state.

This has a pale comparison to the days of the reformation when rich benefactors could pay to get their soul into heaven.

These abuse of indulgences by the church is what led to the split with in the Christian church and the creation of Protestant in Germany and other European countries which subsequently led to some people, especially persons living in Ireland, to leave their home country and emigrate to America in the promise of a better life.

Mormonism is about elevation of the individual but within a closed eco system, where membership and maintenance of your membership and your place in the community is heavily dependent on contributions and part of your income transferred to the Mormon church.

Mormonism rewards people who have been loyal followers and faithful with consistence and continuity of a person's standard of living.

It must be noted that there is nothing illegal about this approach to religion either in the U.S. or other countries around the world where the Mormon church is based, however this does not mean that there is nothing wrong or immoral about their approach.

The fundamental basis of the three major religions in the world is that everybody is equal, even if you are not a member or follower of that specific religion.

These three religions say that members of the other two religion are just as equal as any of their own members and the worshipping of one god makes this an easier prospect even if their gods are different.

The main reason for this is practicality, given the fact that the birthplace of these religions where all in the middle east and more specifically the Arabian Peninsula and modern-day Israel.

This meant for the sake of peace and to get on with your neighbour, one of the tenets of the ten commandments as laid down by God, it made sense not to draw to much difference between persons of a different faith.

And this is how it went for many years until modern day conflicts, the eviction of the Jewish people from Jerusalem by the Ottoman empire and their earlier exodus from Egypt along with their survivors of the holocaust required the Jewish people to create their own sovereign state to protect them from further persecution and genocide.

It is true to say that Hitler program of the final solution created the modern-day wars and destabilisation in the middle east of today which gave rise to the terror groups Taliban and ISIS.

RELEGATION OF RELIGION

The Jewish state of all sudden became the enemy of Islam, even though both sides had been living side by side peacefully for centuries.

It is this backdrop and division, that Mormonism is based in and around, where the Mormon faith, religion and way of life is not available for everybody, but where new members have to be vetted and pass and sort of entrance exam to be accepted into the Mormon community.

This religion is already creating a defined boundary and border for its members and everybody else even before day one of joining their religion.

It could be argued that this is to ensure that they want the right person to join their community.

If this is the case, then the religion is just a front for something else and the main reason for their community is not based on religious beliefs but about the creation of some sort of utopian society, something like you might see in a Hollywood movie, where entrance is only for the preselected and membership is for life.

Anyone else who tries to break rank with the Mormon church or go against their value, is shunned or excommunicated.

They are no longer part of the Mormon community, and they may lose their job, partner, house, and family as result of going against the wishes of the Mormon church.

To followers of the Mormon faith, it is all or nothing, you are either in or out but cannot sit on the fence as to this means that you cannot be trusted and questions would remain over your true motives to the Mormon church.

Many people who have gone against the Mormon church ended up losing everything and have had to move State and start again.

The church of scientology is something like Mormonism in their setup, for the fact that you need to become a member, not just be a follower of the faith like in other religions, to be part of the church of scientology.

Scientology has been known as the religion that attracts the famous followers such as Hollywood star, Silicon Valley executives and mainstream politicians.

When we look at Scientology from the outside it seems like some sort of club attracting people from various backgrounds but similar cultural identity that being wealthy, white Americans or Europeans.

Scientology is not that interested in moving beyond its birthplace in Middle America and this is just perfectly fine with the existing membership base.

All though most of these newer religions are based on some sort of Ponzi scheme formation, that is a pyramid structure, were the longer you are with the religion the further up you go up the chain and the more influence and privileges you obtain.

For any Ponzi scheme to work it normally requires a continuous stream of new members joining the religion, however as scientology is selective in who it attracts and obtains to join its religion, scientology spends a lot of resources attracting membership from the very top of the food chain.

That is the wealthy, old money preferable, white America of European decent, also known as WASP's or white Anglo saxony persons.

Now scientology, will say this is incorrect or factual inaccurate and we have membership from all class of America's, and be able to provide with some sort of proof and literature and books will have pictures of all ethnic groups represented by them.

This is just a cover for a form of socially accepted racisms, creating a religion, club, or clubs where the interests and teachings are purely white person based and would unlikely attract interest and attention from members of any other ethnic group.

It is like golf, if you are not a member of a club, do not have golf clubs or do not know anybody who plays golf, then you are unlikely to want to play golf or have an interest in play golf.

This is what Scientology is about.

Where unlikely Mormonism which does want to attract members from all classes but where promotion and elevation through the ranks of the church is strictly controlled.

Scientology is the opposite for the fact that is strives to attract the top tier of society to their church, and as a result are not seeking social elevation, increase privileges or favours but simply to increase their professional and personal network.

The religion of Scientology is not necessarily about the teaching of its founder but about the congregation of like-minded individual following his teachings in a secret manner that does not attract unwanted attention.

You could almost say that these two modern day religion of Mormonism and Scientology are direct opposites of each other in how they conduct their affairs, attract new members, and see the world.

RELEGATION OF RELIGION

They are an understanding that the top tier of both churches should be a whole representation of all the is below and around them in the church.

Is there any harm then in these new religions that have been created and founded with in the last few centuries.

When people think of new religions, modern day religions, there is a general consensus that if a religion was not founded thousands of years ago, that is one of the mainstream religion then there is a tendency that the religion will descend and become cultish in its behaviour.

This thinking exists no matter how well meaning its founders or follower are in their interpretations of how they should live their lives in balance with all the people around them, with their environment and with the laws of the land that they inhabit.

There have over the last century, being three very high profile examples where self-proclaimed prophets of god have created their own breakaway religion much to the detriment of the people around them, that being Heaven's Gate cult based in San Francisco, the branch Davidians disciples of David Koresh based in Waco Texas, Jim Jones and Jonesborough based in Guatemala, and a bit more different, Charles Manson and Helter Skelter.

Although all these examples are vastly different to the religions of Scientology and Mormonism, they all started in the same way.

This is where a person normally disgruntled with their existing faith, took some time out, drafted a book and created their own religion from which they attracted followers and created their own religion in a rural part of America.

The fact that all these new religions were based not only in the same continent but in the same country, a country that is only two and fifty years old, a newbie compared to most European countries, should not be anything to worry about but why then did some religions, teaching, church's and follower end up going down one path and another set of believers and followers go down another path.

If you look at the religions that descended into a cult, they all share the same belief, that there needs to be an end game, that is something extraordinary needs to happen for them to be elevated to their highest position within the stars or celestial bodies and normally this means death.

Although most if not all religions accept death as the great equaliser or the event that will set them apart from everybody else, that is where those who have been judged will ascend into their higher state, what we may call heaven.

For cults this comes a lot earlier than other religions.

For most of the main stream religions and beliefs, this means living your life as normal as possible, free from as much sin as worthy of living your life, and as you age and you have done all with your life that you can do or want to do, then you should pass, move on or die as the general terminology goes.

However, for cults, there seems to be a general impatience with this approach.

They are not interested in living a normal life, with most cults living debauchery existence, over sexed, over drugged with adultery, incest, and mass orgies common place in their make-up.

They are more akin not with a place of worship or church but with satanic rituals and the being a follower of the devil.

They may be unable to distinguish between living a life that is akin to what Jesus, Mohammed or Moses wanted for his people, but instead intentionally setting out to create a church that on the surface may follow or have some Christian teachings and belief, but in reality is a front for living a sinful existence and following the teachings of the devil in the full glare of god.

It is like giving the two fingers up to god and saying I am making a complete mockery of all that you have taught us and there is nothing that you can do about it because this will only happen for a fixed period of time, until I have done everything that I have wanted to do and then I will kill myself, commit suicide, either as an individual or as a collection of people.

The end game for Heaven's Gate, Jonesborough and the free branch Davidians of Waco Texas, was mass suicide.

When the authorities were going to move in or got suspicious about their actual goings on and activities, they knew their time was coming to an end, they had descended down all the rungs of the ladder, from being devout followers of a god, to being what they set out to achieve, a shell of a person of their original existence.

There behaviour is nothing like of the person they were originally and anybody who previously knew them would be unable to recognise them in their present or end form, and knowing this and that they could never rejoin or go back to their previous life, many decide that their ultimate elevation to the heavens is required and commit suicide, normally by ingesting a poison and falling asleep.

The method of suicide is suggestive that by just falling asleep and never waking up they are on a journey to their point of elevation in the stars unlike other forms of suicide which they may see as crude, dirty and unfit for the state that they are trying to achieve.

RELEGATION OF RELIGION

Suicide, is probably the biggest decision that any one person can make in their lives and thus associating suicide with a form of higher elevation and with the general outcome of cults cause a form of copycat behaviour and it was in the last three decades of the twenty century when a mushrooming effect of the number of cults that took hold and existed was in numbers never seen before.

The hippy culture of tune in and drop out became something different and new cults were being created every other week in America which could be seen as the home of cults in the world.

More cults are created in America that in the rest of the world combined.

What is it in American culture that allows cults to exist in the first place if not flourish.

In other parts of the world, alternative religions are either banned, has no history of existing or is met with deep suspicion.

In Europe, some countries may tend to have cults exist within their country's bounders, but they are either short lived or a closed down by authorities after a brief period.

However, the history of America is about creating a new opportunity or life for yourself, about leaving all that had or knew about yourself in Europe and starting again in a different land whereas few people as possible knew about you.

And it is to this underpinning of American life and culture that cults are playing on, that is people are willing to accept something new or different or willing to give some time to something which may seem dangerous on the offset a go.

To improve their lives or standard of living, they know they must take a leap of faith.

This leap of faith can take many guises, and it may change the person who you are to fit in and be accepted in your new and adopted country.

And this wis hat happened when emigrant from Europe arrived in America.

To be accepted, they change their name to sound more American.

Some changed their religion to have a better prospect of getting a job and support a better standard of living.

Some people turned their back on their fellow country man and only socialise with naturalised Americas or different races.

Some got an education and college degree to improve their lives.

So, America is a country with a history of changing the person you are to be a better version of yourself and so the environment flourishment of cults exists.

CHAPTER 52

Note that it is wise to take a good look at yourself every so often in your life to see if the person you are looking at in the mirror is the person that you want to be and the person you are happy to live with.

Religion's fundamental central purpose is to change the person you are into a better person, a person that God has a vision that you will be.

For the three major religions, this is very subtly done, where normally you are baptised into your chosen religion by your parents who's religion was also chosen by their parents, as so on the line of continuation of a religion is unbroken down a family line.

Most people did not have a choose of the religion they wanted to follow and believe and the set of beliefs that they would instil on them at an early age.

This decision was simply out of hands, hands and they were powerless to do anything about.

This single decision would shape the rest of life, by the schools they go to, the friends they associate with, the sports they play, the area of a city or country they lived in and the jobs and place of employment that they worked in.

It goes onto influence the type of partners they marry and although many societies have open up to different religions and peoples of different background, there is some innate belief and understand that we should stick to what we know and our background that we have come from and grow up in.

In relationships were people married into vastly different societies, makeups, and cultures not just on religious grounds but also from different continents and countries, the novelty of this meshing of two distinct cultures wears off after a few years and the relationship is doomed.

If there is nothing else to bind two people together beyond the novelty of their culture, that is similarities as opposed to differences, then there is no depth to the relationship and no stable foundations on which to build a relationship on.

Relationships are all about exploring these similarities and take them to a different level together.

It is not about sharing what you have done already as an individual or in a different relationship but about finding a partner who understands you for the person you are, the flaws you have but also the effort you make to address your own personal shortcomings.

In relationships, no matter how difficult the times you are going through, once you are trying, the other partner will stick by to see what the fruits of you labour and efforts turn into.

They would find it difficult to end a relationship with a person only to find out that will a little more time, this person turns into something worth holding onto.

Managing relationships is what life is all about and managing your relationship with God should be no different.

As religion and you relationship with god is about change, then religion can be a powerful force for change in anybody's life and it seems that modern day religions are able to take people who feel dejected or unwanted by their own religion and through conversion or baptism are brought into a new religion, family and community.

Most of these newer founded religions do exactly want they say on the tin and should not make you feel suspicious.

They are normally setup by well-meaning people, who just want a better life and existence for themselves and their family and are just encouraging the people who are at the same point of realisation in their lives.

So are all newer religions about creating a community using religion or is there a much deeper meaning to them.

The practicality or the immediacy of most people's lives and the relatively short time span that these newer religion have been in existence and their reasons for being set up and in order to attract followers and believers, is setup in such a way that people see immediate results when joining religions.

That means the reasons for joining these church's must be addressed straight away.

If they have completely fallen out of religion altogether and see no benefit with continuing their religion with their incumbent faith.

If they are going through a tough time in life, unable to find a job, not too many friends, no social life, no family or just no support network.

They feel by joining this new church and they will immediately see change for their better in their life, that is by meeting new people, new opportunities open up for them by being invited to social events, getting a new job or promotion or meet a new romantic partner who will help them navigate their new way of life together.

RELEGATION OF RELIGION

And this is what a lot of what new churches and religions are about.

They are a sort of help centre for people whose life may be in difficulty and many of these church's specifically employ people who make it their business to help followers of the church by creating interactions between new members and existing members.

New members are invited to social events which helps them interpret the teaching and writing of the church's founder and founding beliefs.

These people smooth the transition of new members to the church.

In the three major and what we could call traditional religions, a teacher, priest, vicar, Rabbi, or man of the cloth would normally do this.

In these newer religions, lay people are hired to perform this function and they may be assigned quota or other KPI's in which they must meet in a monthly or quarterly basis.

That is the number or amount of people they got to attend an information meeting about this religion, to show some general interest in the church or most importantly to convert or join the church all together.

The business of religion is far more front and centre with these newer religions than with the three major religions.

Although most of these new church are somewhat Christian based, a new form of religion, that is returning to humanities roots and basing religion on what we can see as opposed to what we cannot see, the question of the need for faith as opposed to practicality is now more in vogue than before.

As the warnings of the effects of globalisation becomes more obvious, people see that a return to religion based on nature, where most religions came from is what is called for.

Religion based on faith really came into existence when it could not be explained what happened when a person dies.

The whole concept of the underworld and then heaven was born.

That is, we cannot see of something is real, we can only believe that it is real and use of faith to back up or beliefs.

Before the question of death needed to be address, religion was based around the season, celestial bodies in the night sky and the growing of crops, the migration of animals.

Through understanding and following these patterns, people could lead more productive lives, hunt for animals when they knew their migration pattern such as the bison of north America, plant seeds sowed at the right time and harvest them near the end of the season with the most light would yield the best and more abundant crop.

All early age hieroglyphics are based around animals, the sun, stars and constellations, features of nature such as rivers and valleys or other representation of the world around these early aged humans.

Nature helps humans and human rewarded nature back by respecting her routine, praying and offering up gift after bountiful harvests, only killing the number of animal they needed to survive and ensuring that they were not over hunting, bathing in her waters and living in one existence with nature.

This relationship further evolved when these drawings where reinterpreted and reapplied to existing relationships between humans, that is the sun represents the oldest male of the family, the rivers and valleys represent female anatomy, large harvest represent wealth and happiness, animals represented males and their anatomy with strong bulls representing males.

Some animals were seen as being feminine and other animals as being masculine.

This association is still made today, even though all animals have both sexes.

Agricultural equipment such as spade and forks evolved into instruments of war and would go onto to be pick axes, axes, knives, bats, and anything you could swing at another person.

Instruments of war evolved from farming equipment as man needed weapons first for hunting and then for protection against wild animals, where man had tracked animals for hunting and food purposes.

The basis of religion is more strongly associated therefore with what is around us not what is above us, with what we can see, hear, and taste, not with what we cannot see but instead must believe is real and exists.

So why did religion transition from the rewarding of nature for bountiful harvest to a following of a faith based on somebody else lessons as opposed to our own knowledge and understanding of the world around that was being pass down by generation to generation.

Once we had reached the limitation of the world around us, we started to look around and wonder what else is out there.

RELEGATION OF RELIGION

The basis of Christianity and Jesus being sent down to earth from heaven was to purge the world of sin and thus original sin created by eve disobeying gods' commands.

Even in the garden of Eden, special significance is placed on nature and a bountiful harvest when eve eats from the tree of knowledge.

The tree can only represent mother nature as opposed to God and the tree of life can only be, her offspring.

Maybe if eve had eaten from the tree of life as opposed to the tree of knowledge, she would not have been thrown out of the garden of Eden and there would have been no need to send Jesus, the son of god down to earth.

However, eve ate from the tree of knowledge, her actions were not to quench her hunger, as their garden was bountiful in many different fruits and vegetables, but she wanted to know what god new, a bit of an Icarus moment, eve knew knowledge was power and for her to ascend to the gods she needed to think like them.

The tree of knowledge moment is the moment in religion and history when the role women played in man's evolution and the growth of society, and the development of man was relegated.

Womenkind had been tainted and has never really recovered to this day, nobody can really explain why there exists a gender equality pay gap, which is why do women get paid less than a man for do the exact same work.

There is no formal explanation for this, with the only possible logically explanation is that in some way and in some peoples eye's, women are worth less and valued less than their male counterpart, and this can only stem from the existence of original sin and how eve went against gods wishes.

The actions of eve in the garden of Eden may play well for any male agenda that exists out there and this is only exacerbated by the life of Jesus and how out of the twelve disciples that he choose to lead his teachings after his death, none were female.

If Jesus was indeed sent to cleanse the world of sin and that being of original sin, you would think that it would be wise and prudent to have at least one of his disciples being female at least to understand the ways of females lives around him.

And it is from this decision that the Catholic church hierarchy is completely male dominated with nuns and mother superiors seen as the role of care givers and not moving beyond that role.

It seems after thousands of years, the position of women within the Catholic church is still the same.

Even in Jesus's daily life he was met by fallen women, women who sinned daily through selling their bodies, women who are begging, are poor, or are adulteries.

The life of Jesus is more about putting the life of women on show as opposed to solving any of the problems associated with their lives.

Eve has sinned and as far as the work of Jesus is concerned, only through his self-sacrifice can the world be cleansed of sin for all of humankind, note all of humankind, not womankind or society in general.

Reviewing the life of Jesus through the writings of his disciples, we can see that the religion that Jesus is creating from the offspring of Judaism is very much male dominated where the female of the species very much controls the religion of Judaism.

In Judaism, women are the main decision makers of the hierarchy of the church and the teachings of the religion.

Men are seen more in the operational roles; were they act and respond according to the sisterhood that controls the Jewish religion.

And this is what Judaism is, a sisterhood were the bloodline can only continue through the female line and not the male line.

This is the complete opposite for the Catholic church, the largest Christian church and true for many of the other churches of Christianity, Such Presbyterian and Anglican.

The Christian church was thus established to be a brotherhood and is to this day.

The Christian church does not see the need to change in anyway in response to modern influences as it is still fulfilling its reason for its creation, that is to provide and support the spiritual needs of its follower with a male agenda at its core.

All hierarchy of the Catholic church is male and even though other churches of Christianity have opened their ranks to females, you feel that they need to give a free role to make the changes and implementation that would really have influence.

Instead women are used as tokens, so that the Protestant churches can say, look we support women as they can now join the church as women of the cloth and can elevate through the ranks accordingly to be Arch Bishop of the most powerful dioceses, which in case of England, would be Canterbury.

Even as the Queen of England was the head of the church of England for the entirety of her reign, it did extraordinarily little to elevate the position and role within the society than the Queen and her realms live in.

Pay gaps and inequality still existed, women not being promoted or hired based on their sex.

And this continued and stayed the same throughout her reign as Queen.

Even though the role of the Virgin Mary, her importance is never undermined by gospels and teaching, that is that Jesus can be born into the world free of all sin, it seems that this fact is quickly forgotten and man's importance is front and centre from then on through all Jesus interactions afterwards and up until his death.

Women have taken a predefined back seat in the development of the Christian religion to the extent that they are completely left out of any lessons or teaching that will promote this role and rank within society.

In Judaism, women's role is about power and control to the extent that the state of Israel has been shaped by female influence from its very inception.

The state of Israel, even though it projects a male asteria, is still controlled by female influence based on it being the homeland for the Jewish people.

This runs counter to the religion of Christianity which also sees that state of Israel as its birthplace of the religion.

In the religion of Islam, women are seen to be portrayed as second class citizens within their own country, whether it is in Saudi Arabia, Afghanistan Iran

Women are seen as the primary care givers of the family and that the man makes all the weighty decision, in the family or the society that they live within.

This could not be further from the truth and Muslim women are very influential within the societies and countries that they live within.

The Koran does not make distinction or limitation based on sex's but merely says the role that each of the sexes can occupy and fulfil within a community and society.

It is not about a brotherhood or sisterhood but about the teachings of a prophet and how through the teachings of Muhammad how each good Muslim can elevate their existence and improve upon the situation that they live.

It seems that some of the short fallings of Christianity is included and enacted with the faith of Islam.

Where Christianity tries to improve the lives of their followers, some of this good intent is lost through political situations, decision-making process, politics, or greed.

Where Judaism brough us the ten commandments, that we all know about but failed to enact in our lives, and Christianity brought us Jesus, who through his teaching we could see the world around us in a different way and actual improves individuals lives.

The religion of Islam built on the lessons learnt through these two earlier religions and realised, that for a religion to make a real impact and difference in people lives, it needs to as relevant a hundred years ago as it is today and into the future.

It needs to put aside petty difference that exist between people from the same culture or ethnic group and bring teachings and lessons to a large population that they will be able to implement and use in their day to day lives.

Muslim people, although the discipline of praying is an important part of their identity in being as Muslim it is not the be all and end all or the characteristic that defines a Muslims overall identity.

The acts and way they live their life is the ultimate guide to being a Muslim and how a Muslim lives their life defines their position within the hierarchy and structure of the Muslim community and society.

That is good things come to good people, and this is the defining message of Islam.

In order to live the way of the prophet Muhammad, you need to be able to live by his lessons and teachings, and this is very much true regardless of whether you are a man or woman, if you live a life that is true and honest Muslim life then you will be rewarded accordingly.

There is no barriers, separation or deviation based on what sex you are but there are barriers, separations and deviation if you do not live your life according to the prophet Muhammad.

RELEGATION OF RELIGION

If you go to any Muslim country, as a foreigner you are expected to respect the religious laws as much as the civil laws, and in some circumstance, religious laws take precedence over the civil laws of the society.

This is because, Muslim people recognise the benefits that exist with living pure lives as opposed to civil laws which are normally created based on the law of precedence.

That is if such an event occurred, and as a result to stop this from happening again, we must create a law to stop it happening and an associated punishment system.

For a Muslim society, by living a pure and moral life, then there should be no need for a legal system and in many Muslim countries the legal system is not that developed as western societies as either the act itself is deemed not worthy to commit in the first place or the punishment could be death.

Muslim countries societies are because nobody should be ignorant of the teachings of the prophet Muhammad as opposed to nobody should be ignorant of the law.

If a Muslim person is going to commit what may be called sin, by simply drinking alcohol, then they are going to commit other sins.

Not that these sins or infractions would be any worse, but this person is simply not living a life that will pertain them to be a good Muslim but instead will continue to commit other infractions and the list will grow and grow.

For a Muslim society, it is simply easier to nip this problem earlier in the bud instead of allowing it to develop into something worse that may also bring down other people of the Muslim faith.

This is why the punishment in Muslim countries for what we see as simple in fractures of the law is far higher and that is see in countries like Iran where a women can be stones for not wearing her hijab.

Sometimes it would be the case that ordinary people take the law into their own hands and punish these people in absence from any authoritarian figure or person.

This is quite prevalent in Muslim countries and especially in what people see as lawless Afghanistan were to earn the ire of the Taliban will almost mean certain death for all those who go against their will.

It would be an insult to other religions to say that Islam is an evolution or refinement of the major religions that came before it such as Judaism, Christianity and the label that we associated with all other groups of prehistoric religions, called pagan gods.

However, it is true to say that Islam has had a look at earlier religions and established a religion that has taken what works and left out what does not work.

The major one is that the religion of Islam works in tandem with a person's life, not against it, not confined to time, place or festival but should be strongly associated with the daily routines of all Muslim people.

It should be second nature to pray to Muhammad, obey the teachings of the Koran and respect fellow Muslim as much as they respect you.

This closely matching of state, a person's rights as an individual and the teachings of the Koran one of the reasons why you see substantial amounts of conversions of Christians to Islam.

The twinning of the religion to an individual's life without any showmanship or need to elevate the religion to a state for a temporary period is not required.

During the holy period of Ramadan, which changes every year, Muslim are taught and teach themselves self-discipline, which is fast and abstinence.

This was seen in the Christian church in such a large scale and affected such a large population, in the early part of the last century but has died out.

Where to go without something teaches you the discipline of appreciating something when you have it.

In the holy period of Ramadan, Muslim 's fast during daytime and can only eat after dusk.

This may seem like a simple concept and something that should be easy to do but try applying this to western cultures in the twenty first century and you will be sadly disappointed.

Yet it is something that is desperately needed now in western cultures, where people's self-discipline and self-worth is sadly lacking and the entire world of consumerisation and instant gratification has taken over and in some way is running riot.

CHAPTER 53

People nowadays in western culture are controlled by advertising companies and big business whether they know it or not.

They are told where to eat, what to were and even how to think and this conditioning of society is the direct result of people not given the time or space to tune out and think for themself without interference from other people's influence and way of thinking.

And it is other people's thinking that is causing the sameness to exist across continents and countries.

If you go to any major capital city around the world, you know what to expect, the same fast-food joints, high boutique clothes stores, sports shops, internet companies and so forth.

What is being created around the world is cities that are templates of each other.

The new compensation factors are entrepreneurialism.

Big business and governments recognising that everything was starting to look the same, with no innovative ideas coming forward and just like a talk radio with thirty-minute loop cycles, people and trends were starting to repeat themselves on every shorter cycles.

The main Christian holidays of Easter and Christmas were arriving earlier every year and these holiday season become the bread and butter of most business was slowing changing.

This was recognised and realised something needed to change, so the idea of entrepreneurship was borrowed from Silicon Valley and Banks and other Financial Institutions got behind this idea by sowing the seeds of entrepreneurship into society, the start-up culture was born.

However, when we look through the types of start-up companies that are being created a lot of them are based on the same technologies with little deviation between one and another.

This can be directly attributed to the fact that people are not giving any space to develop as individuals.

Usually, people went to college and university to develop more as an individual and to understand more about their likes and dislikes and what they wanted from their lives.

Nowadays, as college degrees are shortened and compressed, college is now about quota and get numbers through and graduating for the workplace with hopefully with a skillset that they can use and will be of benefit to society.

In a less complicated and noisy world in the early part of the last century and previous centuries to that, life was nowhere near as complicated.

People had plenty of time to look around and enjoy as opposed to endure life as they went along.

Now if we all lived in a society that once a year for a nearly a month required us to be more disciplined and self-aware of our own needs and the needs of those around, then we would have the time and space to understand ourselves a lot better and be able to be of more benefit to the society that we live in.

And Ramadan is s fundamental part of every Muslims calendar and respect for Muhammad and their own society.

For Christians, holy week was once this time, when all Christians took the time to reflect on their lives and see where they were going.

However, the mass consumerisation of Easter, from Easter eggs to Easter bunnies, Easter is now just a bit if a joke and a holiday and its religious significance is sadly lost.

People no longer practise fasting and abstinence in the same numbers as they did before.

Children and adults no longer plan what they are going to give up for lent or what religious ceremonies they are going to participate in.

This time is a time in the Christian calendar for the purging of one, attendance to confession, mending of relationships and general reflection is what the period of Easter was once about.

Just like All Saints and All Souls Day in November and the holiday of Halloween in October is about respect for the dead and the end of the farming calendar and the onset of the season of Autumn.

All these Christian festivals that were once rigidly fixed in the calendar of each Christian is sadly lost with time.

The number of lapsed Christians grows every year and it has come to the stage for many that they have even forgotten the relevancy of the religious holidays and instead are about planning what presents they are going to get for such a person, many of the people in their lives play a very insignificant roles, but their own importance is inflated if they feel the need to buy presents for many people.

These people feel popular and wanted.

This trend is nothing new and the loss of Christian and Jewish holidays, which were founded on religious doctrine to consumerisation is nothing new and was a trend that was flagged many decades ago.

However, it has been replaced by something that is hollow, shallow, and irrelevant in most people's lives.

Its impact is negligible and days after the holiday ends, people return to their routine even more cynical about holiday and question their participation in next year's holidays as result.

They are getting nothing new out of the holiday, and each year is just a template of the previous years.

It is like all the goodness associated with this period is being sapped out of it and all that is left is a shell of the religious holiday, which is pale in significance to what it was in times gone by.

For Christmas, which is the largest single religious festival of all the religions combined, Christmas trees, decoration, carol singers, Santa Claus and the traditional of gifting are all symbols of the birth of baby Jesus, yet it is almost like Jesus, Mary and Joseph and all the other significant participants in the birth of Jesus have been white washed from the holiday.

The link or associated between the spirit of gifting and the three wise men, carol singers and the choir of angel singing Jesus arrival, or decorations and the illumination of the north star to guide visitors to Jesus crib has been completely obscured by consumerisation and mass media.

This causes loss of association and with it has also lost relevance for the holiday and when after people speak of lethargy for the holiday it is because they do not see the history, relevance, association or need for this religious holiday in their life.

Big business can only go so far when putting on the Christmas holidays.

The real main players for the Christian holidays is the church's and cathedrals where people still congregate not for a good time but to celebrate the birth of their saviour and person who will guide them out of the dark or unenlightened times to a place which the life of the individual is more valued and celebrated.

In Jerusalem, where the three major religions live side by side, at Christmas time the Christian church dominates the proceedings, when normally the Jewish holiday of Hanukkah has ended, the true sense of Christmas is not lost as the roots of consumerisation are not allowed to grow in the home state of Judaism.

Here, the mass showing of the consumerisation is either not aloud or does not have the same traction as it would in other parts of the world.

In Jerusalem and all the holy sites of Christianity, Christmas is almost unplugged, the excess has been removed as just as Easter, the story of Jesus birth or death is reenacted, understood, and celebrated as it was done centuries before.

The noisy of consumerisation has been removed, and what we are left with is a true understanding and reflection of what Christianity is in its most simple form.

So why this disconnects between the birthplace of Christianity and the rest of the world.

Even in Rome, the seat of the head of the Catholic church, Christmas is very much celebrated in its modern form, however it is not allowed get beyond a point where people forget the true meaning of Christmas.

This simple answer is that people are unable to dig deep and connect with the spirit of Christmas on a deeper level than what is on offer by big business.

They do not see the need to pray or visiting a church or giving time to something other than the spirit of gift giving which is what sums up most Christmas for people in various countries around the world.

The geographical spread of religion around the world and the political structure and makeup of the various ethnic groups and diversity as well as the laws and how a country is ruled has a lot to do with religion and certainly in the foundation of a country.

The largest empire that ruled Europe and parts of Asia and Africa was the Roman empire and how their way of life was based around their pagan gods.

They had gods for everything from wine to love and the Caesar in many eyes was seen as an extension of these gods.

When the senate wanted to change Rome from a dictatorship to a Republic many saw this as an attempt to create a ruling class based on the existence of gods.

RELEGATION OF RELIGION

If Rome were a completely pagan society with no gods, something like the Soviet Union during the cold war, it is unlikely that the members of the Roman senate would have had the step or approach to even suggest a Republic.

The next ruler or Caesar was normally selected from the Roman empire as they were required to have a military background as most of Rome's power was based on invasion and control of foreign lands.

Religion was an important part of this way of life.

Many saw the creation of the Roman republic as the creation of modern-day politics, even if democracy was born in Greece.

This is because, politics is not seen as something clean cut, like a military junta would create and control, but instead a collection of men hell bent on climbing the social ladder at any cost, using various malicious mechanisms and approaches, including betrayal, backstabbing, bullying and domineering behaviour.

This behaviour seemed to have been confined to the Roman gods, but somehow the creation of a Roman republic has elevated some people's opinions of themselves, and this is the case even to this day.

As states and countries that where created through wars, marriages or rebellions, and where religion or the presence of gods created a sort of buffer from the real world to the imaginary world, that is man was only accepted to behave in a certain manner and that was not in way to see himself as some mortal or godly state.

As a result, the world seemed to be a more understanding environment, however when this natural or artificial buffer was removed or dissolved, man started to see himself in a completely different light and started to act or pretend to act in a godly manner.

Now modern-day politics, where once the various church's ruled supreme overall, it is now full of people with their own agenda and lack any real direction and leadership.

Even when the Kings and Queen sent Spanish conquistadors to the America's it was not only to expand the Spanish Kingdom oversees, plunder wealth of gold and diamonds but also to bring the Christian religion to other parts of the world.

The Spanish king knew that if the natives of the Spanish colonies converted to Christianity from their pagan gods, they would be a lot easier to control and manage in the long term.

To these days, these areas of the world as Spanish speaking and Christian faith-based society, and in the former Portuguese colony of Brazil, Christianity is fanatism, and they are staunch supports of the Catholic church.

It is a great debate that if Spain went like England during the reformation period and became a protestant faith society, would this have also extended to the Spanish colonies, would the Spanish King and Queen have been as eager to spread the religious faith of Protestant given that it is a religion based on the split from the parent church, that is the head of the Catholic church based in Rome.

And this is a point that needs to be made that the Protestant religion and other Christian based religions that are not directly affiliated with the Pope are sub religions of the Catholic church as the seat of Saint Peter, that is the first Pope is in Rome.

When we mean the seat of Saint Peter, we mean Saint Peters church in heaven where he decides who is allowed in heaven or who must stay in purgatory or return to earth or even go to hell.

Judgement is one of the most important parts of the Christian faith-based system and religion as it is the act or renewal or getting into heaven that elevates the religion into other worldly.

The basilica in Rome is where saint Peter is buried, and it is saint Peters blood line that all successive Popes have been chosen from.

They are not just gods' disciples but followers and descendants of saint Peters.

The doors of Saint Peters Basilica in Rome are representative of the gates of Heaven, and the Pope is the guardian of the faithful and believers.

The Pope message is always about forgiveness and even in times of war the Pope will appeal to both sides to mend their difference as this is the only way to get into heaven is through forgiveness.

CHAPTER 54

The religions that broken away from Catholic church in Rome, are based on reinterpreting the bible and the word of God in way that will appeal to their own sense of how the world should be and look like.

For them, the bible is the Alpha and Omega as it holds all the teachings of Jesus when on the earth.

However just the breakaway religions reinterpreting the bible for their own benefit, the bible is just a selection of stories of Jesus life that scholars many years ago thought is a good representation of Jesus life.

The stories contained in the bible have been chosen by man not God as a representation of god's work and it is not until we put all the piece of Christianity together do, we fully understand the story of Christ in its entirety.

By simply just solely referring to the bible for all our teaching we are not getting a full rounded version of Jesus and missing a lot of points and teachings.

Protestant as we know was created in Germany and quickly spread to other European countries as many people were against how the church in Rome was being run.

In simple terms Protestant was a rebellion against the church in Rome as many people saw that they were not been included in the decision making process that was being made in Rome and therefore just like other rebellions decide that the only way forward was to create their own religion.

This new religion could only be created from the universally agreed text that every follower of Jesus read and that was the bible.

Many of the mainstays and tenants of Christianity were dropped and a cleaner and more sanitised version was created.

The dropping of Jesus from the cross as the main symbol of Protestant must be some sort of two fingers to Jesus.

A man who died for our sins on the cross.

This act of self-sacrifice is almost ignored or relegated as the most important single act that Jesus committed for us and for his very existence on earth.

As a result, all offshoots of the Catholic church have seen their followings drop in recent years ad there is an obvious distinction between the teachings of the Catholic church and the teachings of Protestant church and this is no more obvious in areas of the world such as Northern Ireland.

There should be no reason for religious divides and differences, however they exist based on historical, religious, and political reasons.

This is because the Christian religion has been used as a ram rod for power hungry persons to extend their own agenda.

The Protestant religion has also been created for rebellion and has created religious divide around the world in areas where these religious divides did not previously exist.

As much as people are entitled to their own opinion on their own political and economic affairs, it is a different story when it comes to religion as the word of god is not up for negotiation and instead should be accepted for what it is worth and what it is valued at.

Anything else is just watering down the text that God wants us to have.

The fact that two opposing religions read from the same book and still have reason to go to war is a step to far in most people's minds.

And this is repeated around the world in other religious divides where the basis of a religion has been reinterpreted to create tension in a region where it has no basis to exist in the first place.

We must ask the question as to whether we are witnessing the abuse of religion in its pure form and if religion has become a victim of propaganda and fake news.

That the true facts of Jesus life and the life of other prophets and religious figures such as Muhammad, Moses and Buddha are being told in a way that is untrue, false, or just told in a way that will extend someone else's agenda.

CHAPTER 55

In China, were their is no state religion and mass practising of any religion does not really occur, you see a mass consumer society that just all it seems is to do is that it wants to overtake the West in every way possible.

There is no slow down or what is everybody else doing, instead, an administration that is soley concerned with economic growth and military power.

This godless state just like North Korea, is becoming not an economic partner but a thorn in the side of other countries.

The days of cooperation and partnership are dead, and China lacks the societal maturity that exists in countries which have a faith based or religious content to their way of life.

Having a religion in a society gives more context to a person life and gives depth to their personality.

If China does start the next world war, it will not be based on religion, ideology or political certainty but maybe based on greed, jealousy or one of the other deadly sins that causes people and countries to slide into the abyss of uncertainty.

China needs to check itself and realise that just like previous alliances of Christian societies in World War One and World War Two against evil.

This could be the same case against any future wars that could cause tensions to boil over in flash points around the world and the South China sea seems to be the next flash point for any future conflict and war.

Russia, which is currently engage in a war in Ukraine, understands the need for religion and accepts their own Russia Orthodox church after the collapse of the Soviet Union as the states chosen religion.

Religion can be stabilising factor in countries and regions around the world when it is used and applied correctly.

However as is the case repeatedly, religion is used as a tool in times of war which is used to turn people of a same affiliation or slightly different faith against each other.

This was especially seen in Rwanda in Africa in the nineties when the Hutus slaughter the Tutsis in their millions.

Although it was based on two different ethnic groups and not religious groups, they did for years lives side by side in peace.

Yet investigations after the genocide trace back the actions of the Hutus to malicious rumours that were spread by the Tutsis were devil worshippers and must be gotten rid of hence the mass extermination of this population.

Rumours and false reporting are what led to this genocide from which it took the country years to fully recover from.

This might explain why religion has taken a back seat to politics in many countries as many people simply cannot trust religion any more than they can trust politics.

At least politics is something that is practised openly, daily and in full view of everybody while many decisions made by the church are made behind closed doors.

CHAPTER 56

The evolution of religion has been a terribly slow process, and it is only in recent years that the church and scientists are willingly to work side by side to solve some of the problems that are currently gripping our planet.

People will no longer accept the argument that let gods will be done to explain horrible events such as natural disasters that grip our planet as if god is micromanaging the whole planet and universe on a second-to-second basis.

The church is now of the belief that they are many disasters that man brings upon himself after being warned by God in previous generations.

And these lessons can simply be boiled down to the seven deadly sins such as overfishing in the oceans is a form of greed and the number of overweight people in our society is a form of gluttony.

There are many examples where god has warned us not to do something as there would be consequences and all man did was ignore gods advise or wishes and went against his better judgement and now we are paying the consequences in the form of global warning.

We did not need to know about CFC's and carbon and fossil fuels to know that western societies were getting greedier and were taken the planet and its abundant resources for granted.

When the industrial revolution came and manufacturing and agricultural process started to be automated, we saw that we were on a road to increase use of the planets resource with little thought for future generations and the problems faced when coal mines closed and quarry's which left scars in the planet were just left abandoned.

Man had taken whatever he could from the ground and when everything was exhausted, just left the scene for somebody else to solve the problems.

And god must feel the same that as church's are being abandoned in favour of shopping centres, as people go shopping instead of attend church or Sunday service, you wonder if gods is not feeling a bit fatigued dealing with a race of people that never seems to learn anything from their history.

The endless cycle of war, famine, tyranny, oppression, racism and all the modern day problems that we have created for ourselves, it seems that we continuously ignore the experts in favour of doing something that immediately pleases us as opposed to doing something that will be good for the planet and the environment that we live in.

We as a race have shown little reasons in recent times why we should be allowed to think that we have a god governing over us.

Man is not on a continuously improvement path where we see the rewards of our sacrifice.

Instead, the opposite is true, we see the slow degradation of humankind in favour of economic growth and consumerisation.

If God is looking down on us at this moment, you cannot help feeling that he must be disappointed with us and all the work that he has put in into trying to make us a race distinct from everybody else.

The question must be asked, why would god spend so much time on one particular planet, when there are so many other planets in the universe, that must be supporting life, and still trying to turn around a ship that is not only pointing in the wrong direction but is in serious risk of running aground.

The answer must be certainly for the Christian faith.

That god has already sacrificed his own son for the betterment of our race, he has wiped the planet clean in the case of Noah, he has destroyed the sinful cities of Sodom and Gomorrah, then sent twelve deadly plagues on the people of Egypt in order to release his chosen people, he was watched his own son be born and be sacrificed in order to absolve man of original sin, he has thrown out his own descendants from the garden of Eden when they could not follow his simple direction, he has opened the Red sea up so that his people can pass to their promise land, he has sent down angels to do his work on earth, he has sent prophets down to continue the work of Christ, and the list goes on and on and still we turn our nose up at all that has been done for us and gone on our daily lives as if this has nothing to do with us and our lives, no this is about religion and I have decided that I don't want to be a part of that anymore.

This decision is not up to us to make, instead we are simply ignoring the facts and choosing to ignore our creator.

It is no wonder that the world is in the shape it is in right now.

Everybody is talking and nobody is doing anything about it.

We are unable to dig deep and look at ourselves and do you know what I am going to make the conscious decision to be a better version of myself by doing xyz.

This does not seem to be a factor in most people's lives.

RELEGATION OF RELIGION

The wars and famines that started after the Independence of former European colonies in Africa in the seventies and eighties is still going on today.

The wars that started in Afghanistan in the early eighties is still going on just in a different form.

The mass migration in Africa, Europe and America is the result of war, famine or people looking for a better life is only exacerbating the problem as people in poorer countries are no longer willing to accept the standard of living that they are born into and instead of trying to rise up in their own country and willing to be basically be sold into slavery so that they can live a poorer life in a richer country.

All these people have been exposed to religion at some stage in their lives, Christianity and yet they are ignoring the basic lessons of the bible and travelling thousands of miles for something that they will not experience.

Jesus led a very simple life and existence and wealth was on offer to him, chose instead the life that would give him the maximum exposure to the people in the middle east and not offering them food or water or jobs but a spiritual existence that they were missing.

And this was the case with Moses and Muhammad who both lived quite simple lives to make themselves more accepted to those around them.

And the piety that Muhammad is still an especially important aspect in Muslim culture as Islam removes the class structure from society in that and rich man would pray beside a poor man, and nothing would be said about it.

In a mosque everybody, in the eyes of Muhammad is treated them same regardless of class, education or financial contribution to charities and to elevate yourself to a class which you are not a kin to or a part of is your trying to close the gap between man and god.

A gap that needs to exist as when people elevate their status and start thinking they are God like or demigod their personalities change, and they become a person that nobody likes.

This arrogant, self-pompous personification of something that lacks any depth of personality.

Are we just now lost sheep looking for an expert to guide us in the right direction.

This is a complete inaccurate statement as we know what exactly we need to do, we have been given all the set of instructions that we need to execute gods plan.

We have been drilled through Sunday services, we have joined this religious following, we are just simply lazy as in the short term we want to do exactly what we want to do without anybody telling us what to do as to do so interferes with our happiness and well-being.

Life is now just too convenient in every way with any wish we want being granted on the internet be it food, clothes, drugs, weapons, women, men are all available on the internet for a price.

Everything is available, everything has a price except what it cost to ignore all these temptations and live a life that is worth living.

Modern day narrative by the media, advertising companies and celebrities does not make it easier for the average person to make this decision and the use of influencers in social media just further distorts an already noisy world.

Now we don't know what to believe and when somebody who we follow such as a sport star, who also is a role model for many other people starts peddling a product not based on his or her desire to use that product but for the fact they are being paid money to push a product, no longer are they endorsing a product but instead selling a false image of themselves to others.

Peoples moral and ethics are failing and failing fast as the celebrity lifestyle that we see on television is the lifestyle that we all aspire to even though it is out of the reach of most people.

People selling products are presenting a false image of themselves just to sell a product.

Their image is being tarnished by being associated with such forms of marketing and sales.

People are selling out to big business at an alarming rate.

They want the money and the lifestyle, and they will go to any lengths to get the lifestyle that they believe will make them happy.

Unbeknownst to them, this will not make them happy or give them a more fulfilling life.

CHAPTER 57

What is the future for religion if so, much of it is based in the past.

The days of religion used to intimidate people to live their lives in a way that people saw as the way god wanted us to live our lives are long gone.

These bully tactics of threating people to eternal damnation and being sent to hell for ever for their sins seems to no longer be in fashion or in vogue with all the major religions.

This approach has been softened down in recent decades, where it was the major underlining disciplinary for the major religions for centuries.

This all seemed to change in the late part of the twenty century, when more people wanted to freely express what they feel inside whether sexually, artistically, or philosophically and their religion or church was preventing them from doing so.

Just like during the times of Galileo and the reformation it took bold and brave people to break the exiting Mold that the church had created for people and for them forge a new path for themselves without completely abandoning their existing beliefs or way of life.

People understood that they still felt a kinship to their religious beliefs, but they felt that they or the church needed to update their understanding and expressing of religion.

In the Catholic church, this came about with the establishment of the Vatican Two council which changed the way how people prayed, congregated and how the church operated.

This update removed many of the old observation of the church such as Latin masses and the priest facing the back of the church instead of his congregation.

These simple changes did bring and bridge the gap between the congregation and priests and did for a while stop the decline of the church however in a few decades when the sexual scandals of the church were revealed, there was a sharp decline in attendance to religious services.

Not to the same extent, but sexual scandals did permeate into the Protestant churches however nowhere near the extent that was witnessed in the Catholic church.

It is like the Catholic church knew that there was something big coming down the line and did everything to distract or cover it up and when it did finally come to the public attention, the charade was over, people could now see what was going on in the church all these years, years in which something could be done about it but many choose to ignore or not even admit to the problem.

It is to this backdrop that unfortunately the future of the Catholic church is painted in.

No longer being the disciplinarian means that the church must offer something that other parts of society are not offering or lacking, and this is offering a different pace of life.

Everything these days are set at a tempo that is fast, quick, and accessible.

Religion is offering people a place away from the hustle and bustle of daily life, where people can congregate and meet and interact at a slower pace, a pace that is more akin to the time of Jesus Christ or Moses or Muhammad.

Where beliefs and teachings meet daily life.

This well could be what the future of religion will hold.

People may for a while dispense with all their technology and convenience and other trappings of modern life and instead immerse themselves in a way of life that is simpler and accepting.

This is either at religious ceremonies, weekly church attendance, or prayer groups.

Most of the major religions are scaling back their involvement in the education of the next generation of society.

As schools get turned over to be either being run by parents groups, education boards or other private entities and churches and place of faith are closed or consolidated, religion maybe more of something that you will have to seek out for yourself instead of being on offer twenty four seven through schools, colleges, churches, Synagogues, Temples or mosques within your community.

It may be the case that if you are seeking out gods guidance and love then you have a genuine place for it within your life and with that this will be something when nourished will grow within your life to hopefully make you a better person all round.

For the long term, this the best approach for all the major religions.

The days of saturation point of religion where it was in your life whether you choose it or not are gone.

RELEGATION OF RELIGION

The days of missionary work and priests and nuns travelling to far flung parts of the world to covert pagans and non-believers are certainly ending.

What we have now is almost an ala carte menu for religion, where people can choose the aspects of a particular religion into their lives, that is where something resonates internally about a certain inclusion or requirement in their lives, then people will engage with their particular faith and religion and engage with their church.

It is no longer the case of all or nothing, that is you must accept all aspects of a particular religion to be allowed practised that particular religion or be a member of a church and this is the church just acknowledge the demands of the modern life.

Such requirements by the church, as no sex before marriage and to have received all aspect of religious doctrine and rights, Baptism, Holy Communion and Confirmation were all ignored for many years by followers of the church and the church themselves, that it is almost like the church is compensating and compromising for its followers.

This do it yourself approach to your own religious requirements seems to make sense now, but this will only attract people who genuinely have a calling to Christ, Moses, or Muhammad.

And this is what the major religions wants.

They do not want to spend times and resources convincing people to something that should not require any convincing.

It should be as plain as the nose on their face.

If we look at the world and universe around us, it is difficult to think that it was all one big accident and there was not a great plan or architecture who designed the world and universe.

If it were just one big accident, the collision of atoms in the universe, then would we have the depth of life that we do have in the universe today.

Would we have all the variations of people, colours, environments, nature, and scientific elements that we have.

It is exceedingly difficult that an accident created all that we know about the world today.

At some stage there must have been some help, guidance, or plan by either higher intelligent life, different life forms or different forms of energy that created what we have today.

And this is what the church may be just pinning its future on, that it is no longer about trying to convince people that God exists only to narrow the gap between God and humankind.

The church may be adopting the adage about quality rather than quantity.

When the major religious look around the world today and remind themselves of all the good work that they did throughout the centuries either by feeding, educating or employing people and the creation of societies and countries around them, maybe there is a general sense of fatigue with mankind that man has not evolved beyond the simple concepts of war and attrition.

That man has in some way devolved as opposed to evolved.

That no matter how much time, effort and work is spent on man that man is simply destined to repeat his mistakes.

And God knew this with the number of interactions that where required through the centuries to righten the ship.

From Adam and eve being thrown out of the garden, to Jesus sacrifice on the cross, to Moses leading his people to the promise land, to Muhammad preaching the words of god, man does not seem to be able to evolved beyond the limitations of his body.

Mans brain is only set for conflict as opposed to a peaceful existence.

The church understanding, that it is quite possible that God has just simply given up on man, which is a legitimate cause for concern and that we have been abandoned to our faith.

It is quite expecting that a father may intercede on their sons behalf to help and assist him on his journey through life and god, who is painted as a father figure, may feel that there is only so many times you can help somebody before you realise that by helping them you are only hindering their ability to grow into the person and people that they were destined to be.

God may have simply said, there will be no second coming of Christ, that as far as he is concerned enough help has been given to man to stay on a path of life and existence that is worthy of life and now, nature must take over and that man must be left to his own devices whatever way that plays out.

Like any good businessperson, they know when the time is to close shop and go home, that is when their product is no longer selling, or they do not have any customers and God is no different.

RELEGATION OF RELIGION

Man has just squandered to many chances for anymore interactions to make a difference and maybe this is why the church is no longer requiring to be present in everybody's lives, just the lives of the people willing to make the change that god has longed and asked from us for so long.

Society is driving and moving life in a direction that most people do not want and maybe Covid was a time for us to take a look at their lives, and some people did make a change while others went back to their pre covid lives.

Now the ball is firmly in man's court in how society moves forward, but you can rest assured that religion will be something that will become rarer and rarer in its visibility in public and will be something that will change people internally as opposed to externally.

It is not that religion will go underground or be something found in back streets, but it will be something that you will need to know something about before you can dive into it for the first time or again.

This maybe the best approach for all parties involved and simply throwing resources at a race that seems unwilling to learn or change is just going to leave everybody angry with each other and making society less dependent on any one religion can only be a positive step for faith based organisation.

Therefore, are we going to begin to see a split in society, were people who want to have their religion as a centre piece and anchor to their lives and other people who do not place any importance on religion.

We are already witnessing this happening and it is the basis for modern religion of Mormonism and to a lesser extent Scientology, were people want to move away from populated centres and start again or build a new religion around a set of ideologies that they believe in and hold dearly.

The U.S. city of Salt Lake City is the capital of the Mormon world and was created for people who had lost faith and belief in their existing way of life either with their church, government, neighbours or life in general and decided to carve out a new society for themself that was self-governed and enclosed.

This is also the approach that most cults also take, where people who have lost faith in their existing lives and world up sticks and move to a location with other like-minded people.

But is this not what America was all about in the first place; people who wanted to leave their existing lives and start again in a new land free from religious and political persecution.

So, what went wrong in the great experiment of America as it is sometimes referred to that require people to become even more enclosed, in a country that was bigger than Europe and where the land is more sparsely populated.

The problem is that when people emigrated to America, they may have left their old lives behind, but some of the things that did work in the old world were not forgotten and brought with these migrants their old ways that worked.

It was not a case of everybody starting with a clean slate but instead people forgetting what they did not like and starting again.

And one thing that was brought from Europe to America was the class system which is still very evident in America today.

In a new country with a new political system where everybody was supposed to be treated equally, that is capitalist based democracy, you had different classes existing as soon as they stepped of the boat.

People where still bringing their wealth, history, and upbringing with them.

In most religion wealth equality is a key factor.

Any person joining any of the major religion must take a vow of poverty.

As wealth and money can be a hugely divisive factor in all religions, it was decided by the major religions that if your focus was on purely serving God, then wealth and money should be of no concern to you.

In order to do gods work and good work at that you must be free from all earthly trapping such as money, sex and all the other vices that exist as these are seen to only slow you down in your search for god and happiness.

As such when America grew it was quickly realised that it was not that much different to European countries and instead of Kings and Queens you had rich businesspeople and influential politician.

All that had really changed was the table wear. Everything was the same if not a bit rawer.

It was from this that religion found its new base in the America's and it was not long before rich businesspeople and politicians saw the need to back the new Christian church that sprung up across the America's.

RELEGATION OF RELIGION

Religion may not have had been as front a centre in America's like it was in Europe, but it was an ever-present fixture in every community across the new world.

Most people who had emigrated from Europe because of religious persecution found that they could freely practise their religion but now as a result they were placed in a class and a community within a city, be it the Irish, Italian, Polish communities of New York and Chicago, or the Chinese and Japanese communities of San Francisco.

This created urban ghettos which were very reminiscent of the ghettos created in Germany and Poland for Jewish people by the Nazi's.

Many Jewish people emigrated before, during and after the Second World War because of religious persecution and located in New York.

America had become a melting pot of various cultures fleeing religious and political persecution in Europe, Asia, and South America.

As a result, the founding constitution needed to be as accepting as possible to allow as many diverse and persecuted people to co habitat in the new cities and suburbs that were created to house them.

So instead of America being this land of new start and opportunities, it had in some way become a sort of upscale refugee camp, where people could do what they wanted to do but could not or would not return to their homeland as it was.

So, all the plans that people made was quickly swallowed up by the need to survive and exist in this new land.

People were not too concerned about living the life that God wanted for them but more like just living a life.

The people around were certainly on the same level as you, but this did not apply to all people across the city that you lived in.

Even people who chose to move to the countryside and take free plots of land to farm did not have it easy and days of back breaking work did not yield an easy life.

As the American society started to develop and people switched from merely surviving to thriving you saw the birth of the consumer society where people's happiness was based on wealth and prosperity.

As a result of the American political system, you had boom and bust economic policies where you had periods of great wealth and periods where the country was stuck in the economic doldrums.

The focus was not placed on saving but on spending what you had.

When a period of economic downturn did occur, this just like during Covid period, people started to reevaluate their lives and see if they were going in the direction that they wanted for themselves.

This is when more attention was focused on religion and newer religions that were been created in the new lands of America.

You had the faith-based church of the Born-Again Christians who believed that they only true way to start again was to be reborn and be baptised which would free a person from all their old sins.

These newer religions or reinterpretation of the Bible addressed where people were having problems in their lives and used extracts from the bible and various parables from the bible to attract new people to their religion.

The America's had become very much a Christian based society like Europe, but politics and religion did not intersect to the same level as it did in Europe.

Religion did define some aspects of your identity, but it did not pigeonhole and limit you like it did in Europe.

Unlike the Protestant church that moved to America from Europe, the head of the Catholic church was still the Pope in Rome.

To be a Catholic meant that you had to still accept the Pope as the head of the Catholic church.

This was different in the Protestant church where the head of the church was based on the geographical location that you lived and worshipped.

This meant that local problems with the church were dealt with at local or regional level where major problems with paedophilia that gripped the north American Catholic church were not being dealt with sufficiently at regional or state level.

It was being left to the Pope and Holy See in Rome to solve these problems, which were being slow to be reported and even slower to respond to.

RELEGATION OF RELIGION

This lack of delegation by the Pope and Cura to solve the problems of the Catholic church around the world was one of the reasons why many people lost faith in the Catholic church, its works, and the teaching that they followed.

Many people simply abandoned their faith or turn to another religion to satisfy their spiritual needs.

As cracks began to show and grow in the established religion of Christianity, you have the need and desire for off shoots of Protestantism and Catholicism begin and new religions based on new spiritual beings begin to be created.

CHAPTER 58

The same issue did not extend to the religion of Judaism as for many Jewish people their religion is their only identity.

This is based on the holocaust where they were sent to the gas chambers purely because of their religion.

The ethnic cleansing of seven million Jewish people is an over ridding uniting factor for the Jewish faith, and it is rare that a Jewish person who turn their back on their religion or converts to a different religion.

The Jewish people and the state of Israel is now probably inseparable certainly in the eyes of the Israeli people and now the international community.

Even though Israeli politics is quite diverse and different versions of Judaism does exist, they all still fight for the right for Israel to exist.

Anybody who goes against this understanding and belief is labelled a traitor.

Lines of division quickly disappear when their national security is threatened.

This was seen in the October Seventh attacks when Hamas attacked not just Israel but ordinary citizens of Israel.

It is obvious that Hamas does not want to be a good neighbour, and it makes it more difficult that Hamas is in anyway a follower of the faith of Islam.

The whole basis of Islam is to be able to live peacefully and co-exist with your fellow man no matter what their faith, ethnic class and beliefs are.

And this would extend to other countries and terrorist groups in the region who have an axe to grind with Israel.

As far as the international community is concerned, Israel is an independent sovereign state with the right to defend itself against terrorists both foreign and domestic.

Any group that tries to manipulate the popular opinion through religious propaganda, war and persecution is not a follower of the Islamic faith or for any other faith for that matter.

Religion in any way should not be a divisive factor but a unifying factor on every level and for every faith-based religion.

It is old hat to believe that these freedom fighters, just like the IRA in the north of Ireland are solely being motivated by their religion but more likely being motivated by their egos and greed.

As we understand where religion has come from and how it has evolved its future is a little cloudy for its followers.

We understand that religion will evolve into something that we must seek out and find and understand when a moment in our life requires us to do so, but with the increase use and presence of technology in our lives will there even be time and space for man and religion to co-exist.

All religions have had battles between the field of sciences in the past and in recent times it is accepted that science and religion can co-exist for the main reason that science has not answered all the questions that still exist about the universe.

In fact, as we learn more about our planet, solar system, galaxy that we live in, and nearby galaxy is we know less than we did decades ago.

In fact, every new fact we learn is like turning a corner and see something completely new and devoid of all the previous facts and laws about the universe that we knew before.

We are still very many novices about trying to understand the world that we live in.

Yes we are brilliant when we can make energy from water, send probes to the very edge of our solar system, land man and crafts on foreign celestial bodies, but given the vastness of space as we know it, going to the moon is probably the equivalent to walking down the stairs.

At the time it may have been great but as we learn more about the world, we realise this is not even a blip on the radar and that we should be pushing ourselves even more.

Science cannot explain all the questions that we want to answer, and we do not even have the tools to start the journey to answer the question.

So for now it's time that we took a reality check and realised that we are not as great as we would like to think and that by conquering things that we previously thought were unconquerable does not make us anymore god like or shorten the distance between ourselves and god.

RELEGATION OF RELIGION

It is fair to say that in recent years the level of arrogance that has existed in humans in everything from sports to business to discoveries and science has been breath taking.

This sudden rush of euphoria when somebody thinks that they have stumbled upon a new discovery or have created a cure for a known disease or have excelled in a sport to a new hights not previously seen has made man somewhat of an undesirable person before them.

In many fields or research, development, and human endeavour it is always important to understand that you own achievements are purely based on the achievements of the people who have come before you.

You are merely building upon the success of others, and this is no different in any field of science.

To try and almost freeze time and say this is as good as it is going to get is pure arrogance and delusional thinking.

But unfortunately this is now common place in our society and what is exacerbating the problem is when people under pressure from those around them, lie, cheat or distort the facts to falsify their results and pretend they have achieved something when they didn't achieve anything at all.

This was seen during the rush to develop and vaccine for Covid-19.

Many of the large multi-national pharmaceutical companies jumped on the band wagon to develop a cure or vaccine to Covid, knowing that who every solved the problem and developed a vaccine would make billions of profits for their shareholders.

Most of the world would need to be vaccinated against Covid.

However, during the development trials for Covid, many of the outcomes and facts were distorted by the pharmaceutical companies because no one wanted to give away how far along they were to develop a vaccine.

As a result, people were being lied to by their governments.

It was eighteen months before a vaccine was developed and it is still debateable to the approach used to developing this vaccine as people were still getting covid even after been vaccinated one or twice against covid, me included.

CHAPTER 59

Science an evolving discipline but we are nowhere near the stage were artificial intelligence and robotics is going to do all the work for us and all we must do is sit back and enjoy life.

Many people are under the thinking that this type of life is only decades if not years away.

Sadly, these people need a dose of reality and need to understand that life has not developed that much since the life of Jesus.

Yes, we may have technology that Jesus did not have, but unfortunately man has not developed at the same pace that technology has developed at.

We are still stuck in our preconditions of the way life and people should be and the use of technology as an assistive aid has not changed that.

The use of artificial intelligence in day-to-day life is nothing new and there is no secret sauce to artificial intelligence.

It is not like the secret formula to Coca Cola.

In AI lots of work and energy must be spent on developing the AI engines which is the set of rules that are used to interrogate the data or training sets that are used.

In AI you are beginning from nothing and building up mathematical algorithms based on the type of information you are interrogating.

These AI engines and rules will vary based on the information you are applying to it and if you try and run nonsensical information against these AI training models you will generate an error.

Data centres hosting these AI engines needs to devote vast number of resources just to develop one model or one outcome to a decision tree structure.

AI is seen as another shot across the bow of religion and the concept of god, as if we can generate an AI model and direct all known information about the universe into it then we will get some sort of answer that will shoot down the concept of the existence of god.

It seems that the cease fire that developed between religion and science is over and now its final time to bury the concept of God for the last time.

It is fair to say that if result in AI is fruitful the next logical step would be to develop an artificial brain from the research that would be based on how the human brain works.

The problem with this approach is that man did not create man, God created man and the need to always leave God out of the equation always achieves the results that we do not want.

We are always under the impression that for man to succeed and excel then God must fail and be defeated.

This is something that we see repeatedly throughout the ages.

There are so many people on the side line that feel that God is a threat to their very existence.

Where this belief and understand is difficult to ascertain but it must evolve from ignorance or lack of understanding the role that God places in our lives and has always been a constant presence throughout time.

We have seen how religion has been used in place or any real power to keep a people or race down and under their control.

It seems that only person these days that has any real power is God.

After all he did make everything that we see, feel, and can touch, did not he, otherwise if God did not make everything then who or what did.

A simple accident is no longer liked by modern science because it makes people feel irrelevant or marginalised.

It is important that research solves the problems about the universe in a way that does not shock or offend people, after all this would be bad for business and universities, and research bodies might lose their funding if they were to publish something that was against popular understanding and knowledge.

Universities areas of research are not funded by large religious bodies, by the coffers of any of the major religions, because as far as the major religions are concerned, no research is required to prove that God exists.

All their proof is in their religious book which is hundreds of years older than any university that has existed.

RELEGATION OF RELIGION

The holy texts of any of the religion can be compared to geographical location, actual accounts of people present and real-world experiences.

The events that are in these holy texts are not being disputed, what people are drawing upon is these events were not guided by God but by a man present in a different time, location, or universe to where these events occurred.

What is being said is that God was a visitor from a more advanced civilisation than what was present there and to these people, this person would look like a god.

It would be like if one of us discovered time travel and travelled back to the time of Jesus with all our technology as was able to travel great distance in a short space of time, send message to people from great distances, possess medical cures for sicknesses, then we would look like gods but in reality we are just out of our time.

It is very unlikely that God was a time traveller as God is the alpha and omega to existence itself, omnipotent and this is the understanding of all the major religions, that nothing happens without God wishing so.

This fundamental understanding created by default, a foundation or platform from which people can build this religion and way of life upon.

This fixed point and understanding, rules out such thing as time travel and extra-terrestrial beings or visitors from another planet.

Gods fixed and ever-present presence means that there is no lying or cheating about the facts and the events as they occurred.

Somethings in life are immovable and unyielding and the presence of a god and super being as the direct result of the creation of the universe is not something about which we can argue.

We are still only coming to terms about our place in the universe and understanding ourselves and the world around us.

We are trying to grapple with global warming, as issues flagged decades ago but now are we only doing something about it.

Our lack of ability to do something until it is too late just shows how unemotional developed, we are as a species and how far we must develop before we are a real threat to the heavens.

Is it foreseen that AI and robotics would be a threat to humanity and all life around us.

As we have seen from the days of Galileo, the Christian church prefers consistency and predictability over accuracy and relevancy.

This is because the word of God is consistency and has been a stabilising force throughout the ages.

Even when in the church through that Galileo's scientific basis for the world being round was correct, few choose to challenge the establishment as to challenge the establishment was to challenge god's word, something that would land you in hell.

Unfortunately, this is something that has stayed with the Catholic church to these days, with reports of child abuse by priests in the countries of U.S., Canada, Ireland, and Australia.

But how is it so that in modern times the reverse has happen, when it is almost seen as trendy and cool to challenge, God, the heaven, religions, and any institute that has been long established but has not changed its ways.

The reason being is that the birth of the information age has given the population the pretence that we are a more knowledge generation than any previous generation and that it is our right and prerogative to challenge the established view of the world in any way possible.

The media, society and various governments have also taken upon themselves to challenge the old guard when the priorities should be in solving real and immediate problems in the world such global warming, famine, disease and hunger, all man-made problems but problems which many parts of society choose to ignore.

Instead, they are focusing their attention on bring down the Catholic church and other religions as they see their presence as irrelevant in the twenty first century.

The presence of religion and the church is more required than ever before as leaders becomes not leaders anymore but decision makers.

They have a plan in their head that they are not willing to share with anybody else yet make all their decisions based on this plan.

This God like approach to how they see the make up of the world is based on shrinking the world population to a more manageable level to eradicate poverty, disease, and famine.

RELEGATION OF RELIGION

These new world leaders are not politicians but instead come from big business, whether it be banking, technology or pharmaceutical industry, they are pulling the strings on politician in government.

They are certainly not listening to religious leader or reading any religious texts, texts that have been around for thousands of years and that have been read by billions.

They see the world in short termism, which is decision that they make are only relevant in the immediacy and are not relevant over hundreds or thousands of years.

They are not leaders but instead people with a high opinion of themselves and their place in the universe.

Unfortunately it is these people that are doing the most damaged to our society and their position in businesses and governments is creating an environment where nothing gets done and anything that does get done is purely for the benefit of themselves and not the greater society at large.

Religion does not distinguish between wealth and power as anybody can sin and the largest demographic group in our society that is doing the sinning is the rich, wealthy, and powerful, at least rich, wealth and powerful in financial terms.

In terms of faith, ethics, and morals they are bankrupt.

They are unable to move past the passage in the bible of the money changers in the temple in Jerusalem.

They see the house of god as a house of commerce not a house of prayer, reflection and obedience to gods will and plan.

Two thousand years on and these types of people still exist within our society even after countless recessions, periods of economic decline and rampant greed, we still see these people exercise their hold over society.

Yet when the Catholic church with its large property portfolio and gold reserve, art collections and money reserve try's to exude its own influence over its followers, property and investments, the church is seen as displaying a bewildering amount of bullying tactics and meddling in affairs that it has no reason to be in.

Yet the Catholic church with the sovereign state of the Vatican as the centre of its spiritual and administration has the right and requirement to exude influence in many other ways than just in a spiritual manner.

It was quickly realised that for man to grow and develop, it was going to take more than passages from the bible and a whole infrastructure was developed by the Christian church at the time to build school, hospitals, convents, charities, missionaries and a city to support gods work.

In other religions such a Protestant, the church saw these needs as the requirement of the government as the head of the protestant church was also the head of the country.

This twining of roles in one church and separation of roles in another church or religion, is what created these two very distinct strategies.

To this day, this is how both branches of Christianity go about their business, with the Protestants church's more based on spiritual inclusion in people's lives where the Catholic church is a more rounded people, by educated, employing, marrying people and while also providing a spiritual influence and presence in people's lives.

This one stop shop for all their needs is how the Catholics church has come to be such a rich and powerful institute and Rome an important crossroads for Catholics to this day.

Was one approach better than the other and did one branch of Christianity yield better results than the other.

The numbers of Catholics are on the rise especially in African and Asian countries.

Africa, in which the Catholic church contributed many resources and missionary's in order to covert people to Catholicism seems to now to be yielding results and in Asia where religion was not really an priority of many people, but instead where more influence by political philosophy, such as communism, socialism and Marxism/

People now realise that there has been something absent in their lives, and they believe that this may be lack of faith or absence of a religious and spiritual influence in their lives.

In China, which is seen as an atheist country, where there is no one religion, after the pace of mass consumerisation dies down, people are looking for something new that will make their lives more rounded and relevant.

They understand that a life that is just simply geared to spend and earn is a shallow life and that they have lost relevancy as their lives go on.

The states agenda to overtake America as the number one goal just a hollow victory and a fight that America wants China to win.

RELEGATION OF RELIGION

America, which even though still a very consumer based society and capitalistic in nature, its people are still from a Christian society and most people's radar in the U.S. know that they have somewhat lost their trajectory and need to right their ways to make their lives more meaningful and relevant.

As we see small segments of the population holding increasing amounts of the world's wealth, we also see an increase in charitable cause or people with extravagant wealth giving some or all their wealth back to charitable cause.

So why do people hell bent on profiteering, increased efficiency and capitalism approach life do a one eighty and decide to enter philanthropy and give away all their money.

What happens to them on the inside that brings them to this decision.

The simple answer is they realise that wealth does not bring them happiness, which is one of the fundamental teachings of all major religions.

They understand after they did everything, saw everything, travelled the world, meet people from different countries and cultures that no matter what you are longing for, if you do no satisfy the internal conflicts that exist within yourself then you are never going to be happy.

You will always be at conflict with yourself and others no matter how many curiosities you satisfy.

This simple but valuable lesson is further enforced when they see the happiness they bring to others when their donations changes people's lives.

They themselves become happy and their lives are more enriched and balanced as result of this simple but powerful act.

We see this happening repeatedly when titans of business, realise that their lives up until point may have been successful and beneficial, but only successful and beneficial to themselves.

They missed the point, life is not about self-enrichment but about understanding your place in the universe and how your skills and knowledge can help everybody not just shareholders, investors, and insurance companies.

The lessons of the rich can be applied to all aspects of society, in that instead of looking for a career that will yield the best salary, benefits or career opportunities, we should be more focused on what makes us happy right now at this moment in time.

Not what will make us happy if we work hard, keep our head down and impress the boss then maybe we will get that corner office with the relaxing view and secretary but that may take five or ten years of self-sacrifice.

Doing what we want to do should be easy and not involved self-sacrifice and as everybody is different, the permutation, combinations, and options out there are staggering.

This is what inclusion of faith and religion allows us to do, to see the world in a different light and gives us a different approach to life.

The sacrifice for others, them doing what they wanted to do at that very moment in their lives has created us the space in which to grow and develop, not in their shadow but in their light.

We just need the encouragement and self-belief to make our own decisions for ourselves and not be so influenced by the decisions that others have made for themselves around them.

This powerful tool is so overlooked by many yet is the easiest to implement in people's lives.

But religion and wealth have been together hand in hand for a long time that people wanting to give their wealth back to noble causes after they have achieved their aims is nothing new.

What is new is the number of newly minted millionaire and billionaires who ensure that part of their wealth is used for worthy causes.

In a time of unprecedented wealth, people realise that no matter how much money they have accumulated something is still lacking in their lives and this gap can only be filled by doing good or at least contributing to compelling causes.

So there seems to be a natural barometer that exist within people where if they feel their lives are going off track or a bit off centre then some natural intuition kicks in and guides them in the right direction.

This direction is towards god and gods work whether they know it or not or whether they can identify it or not.

And this disconnection between wanting to do decent work and identifying with any one religion, philosophy or even political system is where a lot of people are at, at this moment in time in their lives.

RELEGATION OF RELIGION

In the last decades the number of charities that have been created around the world to help needy people be it people with a medical condition, homelessness, people in war torn countries or people in a worst state and place then other people has increased dramatically.

This is to the extent that people in their second career in their lives, who have achieved their career objectives are now choosing to work in charities for less pay and less rewards.

This is purely because of work in the cut throat world of business they feel that they need to cleanse and purge themselves of the badness that is associated with these workplaces and charities is a place that can mend their soul so they can leave this world knowing that somewhere along the line they did some good to some people.

This innateness that requires people to do good when the need is greatest emphasis the point that god does exist because this is not something that we learn but that is something that is preprogrammed into us before we are born and is something that stays with us till the end of days.

Even people convicted of a crime and sent to prison always find God and a calling to a world were religion plays a central part in their rehabilitation.

Even with some religions seen by others as outdated and irrelevant their teachings are more relevant than ever and the message that Christ, Moses, Muhammed, and other prophets brought to us is still finding audiences thousands of years after their teachings were written down.

The word religion may draw negative connotations and understanding for many people but whether you are a Christian, Jew or Muslim, Hindu, Siek or Budda.

But the same message is relevant across all these religions that is the need to look internally to move forward that only by nourishing the soul with an honest way of life will you be able to live a happy life and that everything else is a distraction in the world.

CHAPTER 60

The world is full of distraction that takes us away from our natural calling of God and these temptations are often attributed to the evil of the devil when they are just the make-up of the flawed species called man.

Man was meant to be a perfect representation of God but when this was realised that this could not be achieved then an alternative approach or path needed to be created for man, and this enlightened path or path of self-discovery is what we have today.

A path where through learning about ourselves and the world around us we are set on a path that will bring us closer to God, the original plan that God had for us.

For many people this seems too difficult or impossible for them and they are unable to see the rewards that this path will bring for them. For them, the world is their oyster, and they intend to discover every facit of life.

Although it is important that we do discover the world around us and all the diverse cultures that exist, this is often at the expenses of the other races and cultures that exist in the other parts of the world.

Yes, we want to discover the world around us but on our own terms and conditions.

We are not letting ourselves be guided by others but still to our own preconditions of the world and they people that live in various parts of the world and do not allow ourselves to be changed or influenced by others to the better so that we can see the world in a different light than before.

That is, we are still the same person we were twenty years ago and have done little or nothing to become a better version of ourselves so that we socialise in different circles.

We cling to our school and college friends; we do not move beyond this social circle.

We join companies that reinforce this view, not challenge it.

Basically, a lot of people are stuck in the same life that they had decades ago and are bored with life at an early age and as a result take their frustration out on others.

Their unhappiness is contagious and starts to affect other people around them that, they start to bring down whole communities.

Some people might make feeble attempts to reach beyond their existing social circles and embrace communities and person beyond what there used to, but this may be for a brief period and is just for show.

Eventually they will return to their way of life that they have known for all their life and are happy in their unhappiness.

So, what is it that make these people paralysed to change when all these days changes are what it is all about.

The bottom line is people do not know where to start, they have been living this life and realise something needs to change and the last thing they have on their mind is religion.

They do not see the connection between changing their lives and religion.

What relevancy does religion have in their lives.

The fundamental building block of all religions, either the major religions or the minor religions is that in order to better yourself that god meant for us, on a path of enlightenment or betterment, to achieve a higher state of conscious than before or simply to become happier, we need to be the agents of our own change.

Religion and the set of teachings that all religions give us is a set of instructions that guide us in the right direction, but it is up to us to do all the work.

There are no shortcuts, there are no sneak peeks to see what is ahead for us or what we expect our lives to be like if we follow this predefined path.

All we have is our own self-belief, and in an age of low self-esteem, depression and other mental illnesses, it is now more difficult than ever for people not only to find this path, understand what they need to do and stay on this path as the world around us has taught us that instant gratification is more rewarding than self-sacrifice.

But just like doing anything hard, there is a high rate of attrition to achieving your goals and objectives.

If it is not hard doing, then it is not worth doing in the first place.

This goes with any profession or calling in life.

RELEGATION OF RELIGION

We are often taught to do work that we love or join a profession where it does not feel like work, where you will love to go into work every day reinvigorated for the day.

But you are not taught or told to do something which is hard or impossible because doing something hard means you will not be happy.

The happiness is in the reward.

We do not need to be happy every minute of every day.

Happiness is a temporary state at best and should not be our overwhelming objective for life.

Instead, life is about pushing ourselves and humankind onto the next challenge whether this is overcoming our own internal and individual challenges or demons or address the complications of life in the modern world.

We should not be standing still and patting ourselves on the back, but instead applying or own resources and skills for the betterment of all life around us.

And religion is a valuable tool and enabler that can make this happen.

As an already proven tool that has created countries, continents, organisation, and movements around the world consistently for centuries.

This force has never slowed down but refined throughout human history and is more relevant today than ever before.

As people lose sight of the modern world and all its complications, they see their religion as a safe port in a storm of trouble; a place where they can stop, take stock of their lives, replenish their resources and when the time comes move on with their lives in a more reinvigorated manner.

CHAPTER 61

Today many people see taking class in Yoga or Pilates and some sort of mechanism to replenish their soul and spiritual healing.

These classes are about stretching and breathing.

You are not going to reach a higher plain of existence by mastering Yoga, you are not going to become a calmer version of yourself or a more reflective person.

Instead, you will just become a person who is better at stretching and breathing because this is the intending outcomes for these courses.

They are not some sort of substitution for a religion.

They will not teach you or do not have the infrastructure for dealing with all the complications of living.

They are not some sort of quick fix to resolve a conflicted mind.

They are simply what they were intended to be, no more or no less.

This can also be extended to exercise such as sport, which will help with mental health issues but is not a substitution for real friendship and lasting partnerships.

Each person should see each past time for what it really is not for what they want in to be or what gap they can use it to fill in their lives.

Life is complicated but only because we make it so with all the noise from the life we live and lead.

Each person needs to refocus on what really will bring direction and structure to their lives and it is not a full weekly calendar of events, or a to do list which is a mile long.

It is about bringing our relationship with God back into focus and back into our lives.

CHAPTER 63

What about other religions apart from the main tenet religions of Christianity, Judaism, and Islam.

Asia is the main locations for the alternative religions that is religions that are not about a prophet sent by God but a person of philosophy that Asian cultures can identify with.

Asia culture is quite different to western culture as their culture is not so much about the individual but a collective of people moving at the same pace.

This is visible in China, southeast Asia, and Japan.

The only real exception is the largest democracy in the world, India which has a caste system and is a former colony of the British empire.

India and Pakistan were once one country, but they choose to split purely on religious lines.

Before both religions lived side by side without any conflict which is quite different from the present days were both nuclear powers threaten each other with annihilation.

The predominate religion of India is Hinduism and this religion is based on many gods as opposed to one specific god, reminiscent of Greek and Roman god.

Each person has their favourite god and prays to that god for guidance.

It would be true to say that the world of business has far more influence than the world of religion in India and even as a former British colony, were Christianity was introduced, it did not flourish to the same extent as other colonies.

The Indian sub-continent and its inhabitant are hedging the fact that a god does exist and are playing it safe in case one day he shows his head.

Religion could be said to be superficial, as in it is on show and front and centre and people do prayer to their gods, but the same emphasis in their country does not hold the same meaning as in other countries.

This is because the roots of religion are not so deliberate and intentional as they are in other countries.

It is something that has evolved as opposed to revolve around an individual person or calling.

This is similar in the country of Thailand, where religion is on show and visible and present, but you always feel that there is no real backing behind their following.

They similarly pray to many gods but while some gods may be more powerful than others or more reliable than others the lack of a central figure or one god really waters things down as regarding their religion.

This is something that the Romans and Greeks found and was one of the contributing reasons for the Roman empire converting from their pagan gods to Christianity.

The fact that many gods exist leads to a lack of direction.

There are too many voices all shouting for the same audience.

Too many gods make things complicated for all especially when some gods are there for such trivial things such as food and happiness.

It draws comparison to the Catholic church where there is a saint for every possible human endeavour.

Asia culture just has not evolved in the same manner as other cultures were war, religion and politics go hand in hand, and many wars have been fought purely on religious grounds.

This is not the same for the Asian continent where most wars have been fought on political ideology and sovereign land.

This is true for Chinas war against Japan and Vietnam's civil war which was a proxy war for the Soviet Union and U.S.

There has been a lot of foreign meddling, just like in Africa and in Asian countries which maybe one of the contributing reasons for western religions of Christianity and Islam not taking root like it did in Europe and the Americas, with the exception of Indonesia and Pakistan.

These countries are large Muslim faith base societies may be down to the fact that the religion of Islam is not seen as a colonising religion as Christianity is seen to have done in Europe, Africa, and the Americas.

Islam is about embracing individuality and living side by side with your fellow man not about the need to create conflict and war purely because of a person worshipping a different god to you.

RELEGATION OF RELIGION

China where there is no state religion, people are allowed to worship some approved religions, but religions that do cause tension such as the preachings of the Dalai Lama are banned.

In this case politics trumps any religious or faith-based belief system.

The needs of the many out weight the needs of the few and in China, most of the people's focus is on economic activity not on religious belief.

Although this may change and China flattens the economic curve, it is unlikely that we will see mass conversion to any of the major religions.

Again, another Asia country is happy not to need any religion or guidance from above.

This will make negotiations in the future more difficult with China as cultural differences will be more obvious, and China will not be so easily pacified as it was in the past for international recognition and acceptance.

In Japan, Shinto and Buddhism are the major religions with the Christian church also present.

Religion does play a vital role in peoples live and the presence of places of worship are commonplace, religion is not organised as it is with the Christian church.

It is and ala carte approach as you take what you want or what brings you benefit and leave the rest.

It is not an all or nothing approach as is the case with the major religions.

The lack of a central character or presence again shows how religion can be relegated down the list of priorities for most people.

Indonesia which has a large Muslim religion and the largest single Muslim faith-based country in the world, Islam is very much a central pillar to most people's lives.

This is a country were the Christian church tried to convert people to Christianity but overall, Islam won out.

This is to do with how in the last century, religion was forced onto people who had little choose and their conversion may have been based on them being able to attend a school or get a job.

This is still the case in many western societies were enrolling in a school is based on religious grounds.

In other large countries in Asia such as Mongolia and Nepal, religion is based around the presence of nature as in their lives are very much dependent on the weather, as so just like climbers ascending mount Everest, they pray to two different set of deities, mother nature and their Hindu gods.

It is fair to say that religion in Asia has developed based on individuals every day needs and what they see around them as opposed to a single god looking over us and guiding and teaching us.

Real world problems for them can only be overcome by real world solutions and their gods and religions require their gods to deliver on their promise.

Faith shown by their devout followers and anything good and lucky or good fortune that has come their way is directly attributed to their god.

A god becomes more popular based upon how successful their followers are with gods rising and falling down the ranks based on this measure of popularity.

This basic scale may seem to lack any real faith but in a continent that has been influenced by foreigners, this may have be the only way to distinguish themselves from everybody else.

We have already talked about the foreign influence that Afghanistan has seen in the previous centuries and how their faith of Islam has united them against foreign invasion to become the graveyard of empires.

In such countries as Cambodia, which saw genocide under the Khmer rouge, this was about political ideology not religion and the cleansing of society of persons who had opinions but not the will to execute their ideology.

One person's belief that their ways was the correct way for the country.

A lack of any religion may have caused the necessary vacuum to exist that allowed this genocide to occur.

One man believing that he had power over life and death, which only God does may have certainly been a contributing factor for this genocide.

It is unlikely at this stage that masses of people in Asia will convert to any of the three major religions, but Africa and Asia are the areas of growth for new followers of the Catholic church.

Some people understanding the need for the presence of an organised religion in their lives and no doubt the next Pope may well be from one of these continents.

RELEGATION OF RELIGION

This would no doubt trigger an increase conversion and take up in the Catholic faith.

As much as the faith alone should be enough for person to convert, knowing that someone from your region or part of the world is of that faith with a high public profile will certainly increase followers and church attendance.

And what about the African continent, where missionaries went centuries ago to covert people to Christianity.

What direction will religion play in people's lives.

The Africa continent is made up of people who are naturally kin to the presence of God in their lives even if that god has changed and evolved throughout the centuries.

The churches and religion will continue to grow, and Christian and Islam states will continue to co-exist side by side as there are presently doing.

From the Muslim countries of the north to the Catholics countries of central Africa to the Protestant country as it once was of South Africa.

Religion is an ever-present presence, and their faith is strong in the belief of their god.

Although during missionary times, people were forced to convert to Christianity, just like people were in south America, they have clung onto their new religion and are very much a part of their identity and a sense of who they are.

As such their religion is ingrained into themselves, their culture, and their countries history to the extent that religion has weathered all the storm that has been thrown at the African continent.

From wars to famine to genocide to global warming, the people of Africa believe their faith in God has got them through the worst time.

Even in present times were millions of people are making the exodus and trying to migrate to Europe to escape the continent, they are still not willing to leave everything that Africa gave them and many carry their bible and rosary beads or prayer mats with them knowing this is as much about their future as it is about their past.

CHAPTER 64

Religion and churches do become corrupted by the forces that they are trying to prevent.

For most religions there can be seen as dams holding back the tide of sin but inevitable these dams will only hold back the water for so long and a time will come in the futures where these dams, dykes and walls will no longer be strong enough to hold back all the sins of humanity.

It will not happen slowly as the water start to seep over the top of the dam but in a great storm with huge waves that will suddenly engulf the dam structure and the water will go over the top and flood the land with sea water, making it difficult to grow anything on the land for a while.

For most religions, the everyday, sinical and useless sins that followers of their faith commit just adds up to make religion useless in the modern day.

It is just because man is not mature enough to understand religion for what it is.

It is not some father figure telling us what to do, because that would become unsustainable for everybody involved but instead a teacher guiding us to a better future.

Man's inability to grow beyond his boyish state means that religion is wasted on most people.

They are not getting anything from it and their church or faith is certainly not getting anything from this relationship.

And that is just were we are at a human development.

We are just too primordial in our growth to understand the place that religion plays in our human development.

And this can be said for the members of the establishment religions, priest, bishop, Aman, Rabbi, Popes, who squander money on churches and palaces, when Jesus led a remarkably simple existence.

If Jesus ever came back would be appalled by the amount of money spent on Cathedrals, Churches, and art when many people go hungry, uneducated, and destitute.

In Jesus's day, people with leprosy were the extremely low of the low of society and even this group of people were helped.

It seems these days many people are unable to make time or resources available for the increasing amount of poor and homeless in society.

Religion was not and is not about great displays of wealth and unfortunately this type of thinking has found its way into the religion of Islam.

Very wealthy countries of the world are spending billions on mosques, which are huge, elaborate and highly decorated building that can house thousands while at the same time millions of fellow Muslims live extremely poor and subsistence lives.

It seems that lessons that learnt through the reformation when millions were paid by followers of Christ to guarantee a place in heaven, may be rearing its ugly head in the Muslim world.

The religion of Islam is about what is invisible, and unseen as opposed to what is seen and visible.

Islam is a religion of peace, and the holy book of the Koran is about living side by side with your fellow man.

Although the western world is always at pains to say that woman in Muslims country is second class citizen the reality is that it is the very opposite.

Women do exert a hidden and disguised power across the Muslim world in all aspects of living, however for this to continue this is not broadcasted to the world or even acknowledged by the institutions and the establishments of these countries.

Western countries are consumed by gossip and speculation and lies which distorts the world that people live in.

In Muslim countries, many of which are not democracies and which censorship offices are present, their specific function is to neuter gossip and idle chit chat that cause revolution and wars and topples governments.

Social media was responsible for the Arab spring which led to the overthrow of many governments in predominantly Muslim countries which to this day these countries are no better off and were the lives of citizens is in some instances worse off such as the case in Libya and Syria.

The place that religion played during peaceful times ensured people remained peaceful and docile even if the security forces threaten the lives of anyone who went against the establishment.

RELEGATION OF RELIGION

Other Muslim countries that were more stable, saw what the Arab spring really was, a western backed revolution executed over the internet meant to rile up the young and student population of these countries against their government.

These foreign intelligence services were not Muslim based organisation or had no interest in Islam or the teachings of the Koran.

Their sole aim was not only to bring down the regime of these countries, many which had been in power for decades, but to also bring down the people of these countries.

The reason, the religion of Islam has been blamed for so many international terrorist plots and which was blamed for starting wars.

The reality is the Muslim religion has nothing to do with war or terrorism but instead the religion of Muhammed is being used as a tool of proxy wars between different countries just like Africa and Asia was used for proxy wars between the Soviet Union and the U.S. during the cold war.

The religion of Islam has gotten caught up in something that is so far from it roots that many people are unable to understand its religion and see terrorism and Islam as the same thing.

Fortunately, they are not the same thing, but it does require a person not so easily influenced by the media and what their country says and to been able to see the wood from the trees.

In most case the enemy is not some person in a foreign country that you never heard of, a follower of a religion that you know nothing about, a believer in a prophet and book that you probably have never seen before.

Ignorance remains in the world of the uneducated and the uneducated in this case are people unable to distinguish fact from fiction, the truth from the lies.

So why do people in governments allow this distortion of reality and the truth to exist.

It is easy to look big and powerful when you are picking on someone smaller and younger than you.

The west is simply using bully boy tactics on the Muslim world as they see them threating their place in the so-called new world order.

And this phrase, the new world order has been bandied around for a few decades and nobody seems to know what the shake-up will look like with most commentator saying that the economics of the world will pivot to the east and large Asian countries of India, China and Indonesia which between them have nearly half the world population.

The financial hubs of New York and London will be replaced by the economic, political, and social hubs of Beijing and New Delhi.

But will this really be the case.

Will the wealth of the world suddenly or slowly transfer to the Asian continent.

CHAPTER 65

If so, what role will the established religions of Christianity, Islam and Judaism play in this transfer.

The reality is that the world of consumerisation may have reached a saturation point and many people in the west are looking to declutter their house and apartment with less stuff and thus declutter their lives.

They are looking to make their lives more simple and less complicated.

More people are choosing to use public transport than to buy a car.

Holidaying closer to home then taking long hall trips, avoiding impulse and spontaneous buying, and choosing to save to buy high value product than to use credit.

The habits of the west have certainly been passed onto the eastern economies and citizens of these countries are engaging in elevated levels of private debt, mass consumerisation and less place for religion or spiritual guidance.

Many western societies citizens are looking to return to their lives that involved a closer relationship with God after the mass consumer decades of the 90's and new millennium.

Many people in the west have become tired of this lifestyle, just as many people in the east have started engaging in this type of lifestyle.

To show your wealth is no longer seen as cool, with many rich people choosing to downgrade this lifestyle to something simpler and more tasteful.

Whether this can be directly attributed to a particular religion is debatable, but it is certainly closer to the lifestyle that Jesus, Moses, or Muhammed would have wanted for all their followers.

Large and rambunctious showing of wealth, being snobby and turning your nose up at other people who are not as rich as you suddenly do not have a place in many western societies.

So, what led to this sudden change amongst the extremely rich.

As we have already discussed, many billionaires are deciding to give their wealth to charitable causes instead of leaving it to their families or next of kin.

And this kind of latter life thing is also starting to take hold earlier in these same people's lives in that instead of buying private jets, large mansions, and big cars, they are consciously choosing to live a simpler and more honest existence.

By doing so they believe that they will not become so self-absorb and lose track of themselves, go off the rails or lose the direction that they want their lives to go in.

They can understand their flaws as people even if society puts them up on a pedestal and paints a completely different picture of them.

They may understand the path and plan that God has for them and if they start living a life that goes off this plan or track then they feel they will lose the person that they have become and like.

They may understand that their success is not luck but something that is a part of something bigger.

To cash in early on this success seem superstitious but could spell an end to their good run.

And this is the same whether a person has a relationship with God or not or is a member of any religion.

All they need to know is that their success is not simply about their abilities but about their place in the world and how they interact with everybody else in the world.

Religion can draw many different people closer together to a single message and understanding of the direction we should live our lives and treat everybody else around us.

CHAPTER 66

This book was written not to analyse the religious books of the Koran, Bible, and Torah for religious relevance in the twenty first century.

Nor was it to find quotes of passage that still resonant with people today, which we already know is true.

It was not to point the figure of blame on any one individual or group to explain the current turmoil that our world is going through.

And in the same breath it was not to sell the concept of religion and God to the non-believers or way-ward people of the world.

This book exists explain the place that religion once held in most societies.

How these societies were better off, more stable, more economical, and prosperous when a state or country had a religion and the concept of God as a fixed point and a guiding light.

A place, a book, a set of ideals, a moral compass, and a map for people to follow in the attempt to make a person's life and peoples life more relevant and fulfilling.

As we have seen this that religion, repeatedly has been a force for good in regions of the world, even if it may take decades or centuries for this work to be realised.

In places of the world where pagan gods have been replaced by Christianity, this transition in some case has not been peaceful.

In today's world where the Pope is the head of a global religion, there is union and recognition between countries of this unifying bond.

This contrasts with each region with in own pagan gods rooted in the environment around them.

However, on the same coin we have also seen the abuses committed by the Catholic church in English speaking countries around the world were men of the cloth get swallowed by the evil that they are employed to stop and root out.

The seven deadly sins, often portrayed in films is on full view through the committal of such evil act as child abuses and punishment of fallen women in the laundries that the lived in.

These men were two faced to God in the sense that they went about their lives giving the impression that they were doing god's work when they were manipulating the very fabric of society and the future generation of a country.

We must see these acts as evil with the ongoing war between the forces of good and the forces of evil.

As I draft this book, wars, and ongoing atrocities are being committed on every continent of the world.

No country is safe from the influence that evil brings.

Increasing mass shooting in the U.S., acts of terrorism in Europe, war and genocide in Africa, the abuse of people's liberties and rights in Asia, phobias of any person who is anyway different to you, high crime rates in south America, homophobia in the oceanic countries.

There has never been a time in human history were so much evil is being committed and yet we seem unable or unwilling to do anything about it.

Once it has nothing to do with me then I am not interested attitude.

But is religion a way out of this mess or just a way to cover up underlining issues that have been there and that have existed for centuries.

The fact that Christianity and Islam have taken root in far flung countries around the world and is not solely the exclusivity of the middle east means that their message is resonating to a new audience in different countries.

The battle for people to understand the need and the place that religion plays in people lives, for most people has been won.

People feel the need to believe in something other than themselves or society of their government.

The see many governments failing their people and greed and nepotism running rampant in many countries.

They feel that religion could be a great equaliser for the fact that God and religions see everybody as the same, no difference placed on creed, colour, or culture.

Even though today, many people assume that people of a certain religion look a certain way.

This is far from the truth.

RELEGATION OF RELIGION

Religion breaks down the stereotypical classes that exist and as a lot of current tension and wars that exist in the world is based on how someone looks, following a religion will certain smooth out any of these intolerances that people have.

We understand that religion can solve some of the world problem by following the simple principles that most religions preach but what about the rest of the world problem.

Is it the case one size fits all.

All man's problems are intricately linked in that greed contributes to wealth inequality around the world.

Jealousy contributes to people feeling their being left out of something and subsequently self-isolation, gluttony leads of weigh issues in people and mass obesity in the population.

This can lead to certain countries having half the population as obese which can lead to health complication and an unhappy population.

Every direct action by man that causes harm can be attributed to a sin committed on their part.

It is no more complicated than that.

Yet it is something that the politicians are unable to understand.

After thousands of meetings and conferences held to address one problem or another, the cause and effect have already been known for thousands of years.

All their actions were simply to hide their inaction and laziness to do anything about the problems.

We do not need Politician's, Consultant's or over paid CEO's coming together to try and address the world's problem such is the annual gathering of egos at Davos every year.

Other secret organisation such as the Bilderberg conference has an open invitation to the elite, the so called rich and powerful around the world to try and shape future world events.

Someone has the idea that these millionaire and billionaire are going to solve the world problems.

Just like they solved the energy crisis or created large IT companies using other people's data or insurance companies that sell piece of mind.

These people only know how to solve niche problems, not problems that effect a whole planet.

The problems of the world today can only be solved if first everybody knows what the problems is, and this requires the removal of misinformation or inaccurate reporting by journalist on key global events.

Journalists are being picked on as not reporting the facts of a situation.

While this may hold true it is up to everyone on the planet not to accept everything we read or hear and interrogate the facts before we believe anything.

As the religious text are often seen as directly coming from God or being the word of God, we accept them just like the expression 'as Gospel' and do not question the accuracy and facts behind passages in the Koran, Jewish Bible or Christian Bible.

These texts have been curated through the centuries as accurate reflections of the lives of prophets.

However, when these texts are presented to people, persons need to understand the difference between what man said and what god has said to his people.

We should never try to confuse the two or even accept that different pieces of writing are from the same source.

How will religion evolve, and can we say that religion has failed us or not achieve its purposes.

Religion is the outcome of a visitation of a prophet sent by God to earth to lead his people to a better life.

It is us that has given the name religion, which has organised the lessons and stories into books that latter become the New and Old Testament books and the various texts that make up the Jewish Bible, the Koran, and the Christian bible.

It is man that has built churches, cathedral, mosques, and synagogue to worship our god.

It is man that has organised pilgrimages and that has created the Christian, Jewish and Muslim holidays based around noteworthy events that occurred in this prophet's life.

It is man that has created calendars and follows the days, weeks, months, and years around their religion.

It is man that has taken up arms against other religions in the belief that their god is the one true god and that any other person saying otherwise should be eliminated.

RELEGATION OF RELIGION

It is man that has and is using religion as a weapon for war and has done so for centuries.

It is man that sees difference in his fellow man and allows it to become a point of conflict.

But obviously with all this conflict the power of religion has not diminished and if anything, it is continuously being used as a battering ram for one group influence over another.

Man has taken something in its purest form and sullied it.

Something that was supposed to absorb all the sins of man has become something different and it was the case that religion was supposed to be temporary not permanent as we have it.

We realised it that the power it held, and just like an old man nursing his pint, we have held onto the concept of religion for too long and that its meaning and message has long being lost.

Religion was only supposed to solve a problem or impasse such as original sin, or the cities of Sodom and Gomorrah, or man losing his way ward path.

A sort of plaster situation to cover the wound so that man could move on with his life.

Instead, what we have is a sort of paralysis by analysis.

We are continuing going over the works of men, long since dead and whose lived thousands of years ago.

We are just trying to draw parallels with these good men to give some meaning to our lives and to make us feel better about ourselves.

We have been sold something that has long since reached its best before date.

Yet we clinging to these relics of the past in the hope that it will bring a different dimension to our lives in a world where most people seem lost, unaccepted, unwanted or without direction.

Just like Christians are seen as lambs of gods, they do not realise that their Shepard has since moved on and that they are no better off than they were two thousand years ago.

This may seem harsh to say, but the fact is history keeps on repeating itself and the world is not getting to be the paradise that so many people want it to be.

The fact is man needs to wake up, grow up and be a man not a boy.

Really know what is takes to walk in Jesus's, Moses's, or Muhammed's footsteps.